INDIAN TEACHERS OF BUDDHIST UNIVERSITIES

INDIAN TEACHERS OF BUDDHIST UNIVERSITIES

BY

PHANINDRANATH BOSE

GYAN

Published by

Gyan Publishing House
5, Ansari Road
Daryaganj, New Delhi-110002
Phone: 011-47034999, 9811692060
E-mail: books@gyanbooks.com

Distribution Network
gyanbooks.com
India, USA, Canada, UK, Australia

ISBN: 978-93-6208-077-6 (PB)
First Published, 1923

2nd Impression 2024

Printed at: Gyan Press, Delhi.

INDIAN TEACHERS OF BUDDHIST UNIVERSITIES
Author: PHANINDRANATH BOSE

INDIAN TEACHERS
OF
BUDDHIST UNIVERSITIES

INDIAN TEACHERS OF BUDDHIST UNIVERSITIES

BY

PHANINDRANATH BOSE

(*Visvabharati, Santiniketan*)

THEOSOPHICAL PUBLISHING HOUSE

ADYAR, MADRAS, INDIA

1923

DEDICATED

TO

SYLVAIN LEVI, D.Litt.

THE FIRST VISITING PROFESSOR OF VISVABHARATI

BY

HIS HUMBLE STUDENT

INTRODUCTION

An attempt has been made in the following pages to bring together the accounts of the Indian pandits of the Buddhist Universities of Nālanda, Vikramasīlā, Odantapura and Jāgaddala. I have tried to show how most of them were associated with Tibet, and how they influenced Tibetan literature and religion.

My thanks, in this connection, are due to Pandit Vidhusekhara Sastri, Principal of Visvabharati, for his kind suggestions, and to my pupils Sreman P. Anujan Achan and Sreman Chunibhai Patel for their valuable help. Lastly, I must not forget to thank the Theosophical Publishing House Board for including the book in their Asian Library Series.

Visvabharati
Shantiniketan

PHANINDRANATH BOSE

CONTENTS

CHAPTER I

STUDENTS OF TIBETAN BUDDHISM

VARIOUS scholars of the West as well as of the East have laboured, and are labouring, towards the elucidation of the deep mysteries of Tibetan Buddhism. Owing to the peculiar geographical position of Tibet, it was regarded as the "Forbidden Land" by scholars for a long time. Attempts were first made by missionaries to reach this land of mysteries and reveal the peculiar customs and manners prevailing among the people of the soil. One of the earliest missionaries to reach Tibet was Father Antonio de Andrade, who was born at Oleiros, in Alentejo, in 1580. He belonged to the Society of Jesus. After visiting Tibet, he published a book on Tibet, named—'Nuevo descubrimiento del gran Cathayo, à Reynos de Tibet' (por el Padre Antonio de Andrade, de la Compañia de Jesus, Portugues, en el año de 1624). This seems to have been the earliest publication by a European missionary about Tibet. He was followed by another member of the Society of Jesus, Jean Grueber, who, in his 'Travels from China to Europe in 1661,' describes the land of Tibet. An Italian Jesuit, H. Desideri, also penetrated into Tibet in 1714 and gave his impressions in his book—'Travels into Tibet in 1714'. Towards the end of the eighteenth century A.D. George Bogle also went to study the manners and customs of the Tibetans. His 'Relation du Thibet' (Contenant l'exposition des Mœurs, des Coûtumes, de la Religion et du Commerce des Habitans, extraite des Papiers de M. Bogle, Par M. Stewart) was published in 1778. It is noteworthy that no English scholar or traveller had so far tried to go into the country. Perhaps the first English travellers to the Forbidden Land were Samuel Turner and Thomas Manning. Early in the nineteenth century, the former went through Bhutan. In 1806 he published 'An Account of an Embassy to the Court of the Teshoo Lama, in Tibet; containing a Narrative of a Journey through Bhootan and Part of Tibet'. Thomas Manning forced his way up to Lhāsa, the capital of Tibet in 1811—12. 'The Journey of Mr. Thomas Manning to Lhasa' was published by Clements R. Markham, with an account of his life, in 1876.

The Indian Government also from time to time sent missions to Tibet. Dr. A. Campbell, who was the Superintendent of Darjeeling, tried to reach Tibet. In the Journal of the Asiatic Society of Bengal he published his 'Itinerary from Phari in Thibet, to Lassa, with appended Routes from Darjeeling to Phari'.[1] Four years after, he brought out his 'Diary of a Journey

[1] XVII, pp. 257—276, April, 1848.

through Sikim to the Frontiers of Thibet,' in the pages of the same Journal.[1] In 1848 Lieut.-General Sir Richard Strachey had undertaken the mission as far as lake Manasarowa. His 'Narrative of a Journey to the Lakes Ra-kas-tal and Manasarowar, in Western Tibet' was published in the "Geographical Journal" in 1900. Indians also tried to find out the way to Tibet. In 1867 the Government of India sent a mission from the Great Trigonometrical Survey of India. The survey was undertaken by a pandit, whose report was published in 1867 under the title of—'Route survey from British India into Great Tibet through the Lhasa territories, and along the upper course of the Brahmaputra River, or Nari-chu Sangpo, made by Pundit . . . and compiled from the original materials by Capt. T. G. Montgomerie' (1867). Three years after, another Indian tried to reach the mysterious

[1] Journal of the Asiatic Society of Bengal, 1852, pp. 407—28.

land. That 'Account of an attempt by a Native Envoy to reach the Catholic Missionaries of Tibet' was published by Captain J. Gregory.[1] Seven years after another Indian pandit proceeded to Lhāsa through Assam. Captain H. Trotter, R.E., published the 'Account of the Pundit's Journey in Great Tibet from Leh in Ladākh to Lhāsa and of his return to India via Assam'.[2]

Towards the end of the nineteenth century scholars like W. W. Rockhill, Mrs. Bishop, A. R. Taylor, Csoma de Körös, Waddel and others went over to Tibet to learn something of the people and their religion. W. W. Rockhill produced his famous book[3] in 1891. Next year he wrote about his *Travels in Tibet* in the pages of the "Edinburgh Review".[4] Mrs. Isabella L. Bishop was the first lady traveller to go

[1] *Proc. Roy. Geo. Soc.*, 1870, Vol. XIV, pp. 214—219.

[2] *Ibid.*, 1887, XXI, pp. 325—350.

[3] *The Land of the Lamas. Notes of a Journey through China, Mongolia and Tibet (with maps and illustration).*

[4] April, 1892, pp. 540—558.

into the Forbidden Land and write about it. In 1892 she wrote 'A Journey through Lesser Tibet'.[1] Another lady who followed Mrs. Bishop was Miss Annie R. Taylor. She spoke of her *Experiences in Tibet* before the Scottish Geographical Society, in Edinburgh, in December, 1893. Afterwards, her 'Adventures in Tibet including the Diary of Miss Annie R. Taylor's remarkable journey from Tan-chan to Ta-chieor-Lu through the heart of the "Forbidden Land"' was brought out by William Carey, in 1901.

We must not omit the names of Rai Sarat Ch. Das Bahadur and of MM. Satish Ch. Vidyabhusan, who also went into the land of Tibet and rendered yeoman service to the cause of Tibetan Buddhism. Born in 1849, at Chittagong, Sarat Chandra Das was sent to Tibet by the Government of India. His interesting book—'Journey to Lhāsa and Central Tibet' was

[1] *Scottish Geog. Mag.*, VIII, 1892, pp. 513—528.

published in 1902.[1] MM. Satish Ch. Vidyabhusan also paid a visit to Sikkim in 1907.

The combined efforts of these travellers and scholars helped us in getting a mass of information about the religion, literature, manners and customs of Tibet. Leaving aside the account of the journeys to Tibet, let us now turn to the account of the critical study of the language, literature and religion of Tibet by various scholars. The first scholar to introduce the Tibetan alphabets to the West was Fr. Augustini Antonii Georgii. The publication of his 'Alphabetum Tibetanum Missionum apostolicarum commodo editum' brought in a new age in the study of Tibetan Buddhism. A long period elapsed after this before another serious attempt was made in this direction. The Rev. Frederic Christian Gotthelf Schroeter tried to compile the first Tibetan Dictionary

[1] It was translated into German under the title of *Reise in Tibet*, von Dr. H. Repsold, and into Russian by V. Kotvitch in 1904.

for the use of the western scholar. He, however, died after preparing the manuscript copy of this Dictionary. The Rev. John Marshman of Serampur edited the Dictionary and brought it out with a short discourse on a Grammar of the Bhotanta Language, in 1826. This Dictionary was known as—'A Dictionary of the Bhotanta or Bontom Language'. The Preface of this dictionary states: "It is highly probable that the following Dictionary was written by some of the Roman Catholic missionaries who formerly laboured in Thibet. A copy of it was in the possession of the late Major Latter, which was copied by the late Rev. Frederick Schroeter, a missionary belonging to the Church Missionary Society. Mr. Schroeter was placed at Tentaliya, a military post in Poornea, and received a salary from the Government. On his demise his manuscripts were submitted to the inspection of the editor, on whose recommendation the printing of the whole was sanctioned by the Government, and the expense defrayed by a generous subscription. The dictionary was originally written in Italian, and has been partly translated into English by Mr. Marshman."[1]

The scholar, Alexander Csoma de Körös, was the first to begin a scientific study of Tibetan Buddhism. He has been aptly described by Léon Feer, as "*Fondateur des études tibétaines*" or the " Father of Tibetan Studies ". He was born in Transylvania in 1784. After passing some time at Ladāk, he brought out a Tibetan Grammar and a Tibetan Dictionary in 1834. His book, 'A Grammar of the Tibetan Language in English,' helped the English-reading public to know something about the grammatical peculiarities of the Tibetan language. In the publication of this monograph, he was assisted by the Bengal Government and by the Asiatic Society of

[1] H. Cordier—Bibliotheca Sinica, Vol. IV, Fas. II, Col. 2929.

Bengal. Another treatise of his was—'Essay towards a Dictionary, Tibetan and English'. It was prepared with the assistance of Bandé Sangs-Rgyas Phun-Tshogs, a learned Lama of Zangskār, during his residence at Kanam, in the Himālayan mountains, on the confines of India and Tibet in 1827—1830. A. Csoma de Körös wanted to proceed again to Tibet. Unfortunately he died on the way at Darjeeling, on 11th April, 1842. He was a great Tibetan scholar; had learned the Tibetan language from the Lamas in Tibet; and was the first scholar to begin making the Catalogue of *Tanjur* as well as of *Khan-gyur* in the pages of the "Asiatic Researches". His Catalogue of *Khan-gyur* has not yet been surpassed by any since made. He was also the first to bring down the manuscripts of the whole Tibetan Tripitaka to India; and his collection is still preserved in the library of the Asiatic Society of Bengal. As a fitting tribute to the great

Hungarian traveller and scholar, all his articles scattered over seven different volumes of the Journal of the Asiatic Society of Bengal, were collected and reprinted under the title, 'Tibetan Studies,' on the occasion of the one hundred and twenty-fifth anniversary of his birth. (He was born in April, 1784.) Fourteen articles of varied interest have been collected in that volume (1912). Some of the important articles are:

Note on the origin of the Kala-Chakra and Adi-Buddha systems;

Origin of the Shakya Race;

Analysis of a Tibetan Medical Work;

Notices on the Different Systems of Buddhism, extracted from the Tibetan authorities;

Enumeration of Historical and Grammatical works to be met with in Tibet.

In the pages of the "Asiatic Researches" A. Csoma de Körös gave the 'Analysis of the Dulva, a portion of the Tibetan work entitled the Kan-gyur'.[1] Other important articles of his in the same Journal are:

[1] Vol. XX, pp. 41—93, 1836.

Notices on the Life of Shakya, extracted from the Tibetan authorities;[1]

Analysis of the Sher-chin-P'hal-ch'hen-Dkon-séks-Do-dé-Nyāng-dās and Gyut; Being the 2nd, 3rd, 4th, 5th, 6th and 7th Divisions of the Tibetan work entitled the *Kan-gyur*;[2]

Abstract of the contents of the *Bstan-Hgyur*.[3]

Another worker in the Field of Tibetan Buddhism was Brian Houghton Hodgson, who was the Resident of Nepal from the year 1833. His sojourn in Nepal over a period of twenty-five years, helped him to get into close contact with the religion and literature of Nepal and Tibet. About his works, Dr. Rajendra Lal Mitra says:

> He has done more on that subject than any other European writer. Before his time all that was known of Buddhism was crude, vague and shadowy, derived from secondary and by no means reliable sources. He it was who established the subject on a sound philosophic basis.[4]

[1] Asiatic Researches, 1836, pp. 285—317.

[2] *Ibid.*, pp. 393—552.

[3] *Ibid.*, pp. 553—585.

[4] *The Sanskrit Buddhist Literature of Nepal*, by Dr. R. L. Mitra, p. xii—xiii.

Mr. Hodgson's illustrations of the literature and religion of the Buddhists form a wonderful combination of "knowledge on a new subject with the deepest philosophical speculations," says M. Csoma de Körös. His 'Illustrations of the Literature and Religion of the Buddhists' was published from Serampore in 1841. One most important contribution of his was the bringing of two complete sets of Xylographs of the great Cyclopædias of Tibet, each set comprising three hundred and thirty-four bulky volumes, printed with wooden blocks on Tibetan paper. He presented the first set to the Asiatic Society of Bengal, and the second to the India Office.

About this time France also took up the study of Tibetan Buddhism seriously. The study of Sinology had already been begun, but now French scholars turned their attention in this direction. Philippe Edouard Foucaux was the first in the field. On 31 January, 1842, he gave a 'Discours prononcé à l'Ouverture du Cours de Langue et de Literature tibétaine près la Bibliothèque royale'. After the publication of the Tibetan Grammar by A. Csoma de Körös, he brought out his 'Grammaire de la Langue tibétaine' in 1858. This was the first Tibetan Grammar in the French language. In 1847 M. Foucaux translated the Tibetan version of *Lalita-Vistara* into French. The work was called 'Rgya Tch'er Rol Pa ou Développement des Jeux contenant l'histoire du Bouddha Çakya-Mouni traduit sur la Version tibétaine du Bkah Hgyour, et revu sur l'original sanskrit (Lalita-Vistara)'. A few years after, Dr. Rajendralal Mitra brought out the sanskrit version of *Lalita-Vistara* or 'Memoirs of the Life and Doctrines of Sakya Sinha' (Calcutta, 1853). As Professor of Sanskrit in the college of France, M. Foucaux translated the fourth chapter of the "Lotus of the Good Law" from the original Tibetan—'Parabole de l'Enfant égaré, formant le chapitre IV du Lotus de la Bonne Loi, publiée pour la première fois en sanscrit et en tibétain, lithographiée à la manière des livres du Tibet, et accompagnée d'une traduction française d'après la version tibétaine du Kanjour' (1854).

His important translations from the original Tibetan are:

'Le Sage et le Fou,' extrait du Kan-jour (1842);

'Le Trésor des Belles Paroles,' choix de Sentences composées en tibétain par le Lama Saskya Pandita, suivées d'une élégie tirée du Kanjour (1858);

'La Guirlande précieuse des demandes et des réponses,' publiée en sanskrit et en tibétain (1867);

'Le Religieux chassé de la communauté,' conte bouddhique traduit du tibétain pour la première fois (1872).

Another great scholar, who busied himself with the mysteries of Tibetan Buddhism, was Antoine Schiefner. In 1851 he published his *Tibetische Studien* in German. His best contribution in this direction was the German translation of Lama Tārānātha's "History of

Indian Buddhism" from the original Tibetan. The book, which is a mine of information for students of Indian Buddhism, is known as—'Täränātha's Geschichte des Buddhismus, von Schiefner'. Another work of his is—'Tibetan Tales, derived from Indian Sources'; translated from the Tibetan of Kan-Gyur. (1882.)

In the middle of the nineteenth century there appeared another scholar, H. A. Jaeschke by name. He was born at Herrnhut on 17 May, 1817. As a Moravian Missionary at Kyélang, he was able to enter deep into the spirit of the Tibetan language. In 1865 he published 'A short practical Grammar of the Tibetan Language, with special reference to the spoken dialects.' In 1866 his 'Romanized Tibetan and English Dictionary' came out, and was followed by 'A Tibetan-English Dictionary with special reference to the prevailing dialects' (Prepared and published at the expense of the Secretary of State for India in Council, London, 1881).

We shall now turn to an Indian scholar, Rai Sarat Ch. Das Bahadur, whose contributions to this field of study cannot be gainsaid. Born at Chittagong in 1849, he was appointed Headmaster of the Tibetan Boarding School at Darjeeling in 1874. There he found opportunities to study the Tibetan language and literature. In 1878 he asked and obtained permission from the Dalai Lama to visit Tibet. Accordingly he set out in 1879 and returned after an absence of six months. A few years after, in 1881, he was again invited by the Tashi Lama to visit Tashilhumpo. In the same year he undertook the journey across the Himālayas and returned to India in 1883 with some Tibetan manuscripts. Afterwards he went with Colman Macaulay to the Tibetan frontier. The following year he was sent by the Government of India to Peking to assist the Government in diplomatic matters connected with Tibet.

Sarat Ch. Das was a great Tibetan scholar. He translated and edited many Tibetan works. He wrote a series of articles called 'Contributions on the Religion, History, etc., of Tibet'.[1] The materials for this series were collected from the original Tibetan. He edited both the Sanskrit and Tibetan versions of 'Avadan-kalpa-kata' for the Asiatic Society of Bengal. The valuable Tibetan historical work 'Pagsam Jon-Zañ' was edited by him in the original Tibetan for the Bengal Government. His important articles are:

A brief account of Tibet from "Dsam Ling Gyeshe," the well-known geographical work of Lama Tsanpo Nomankhan of Amdo;[2]

The sacred and ornamental characters of Tibet;[3]

Life of Sum-pa Khan-po, also styled Ye-Ses-Dpal-hbyor, the author of the Rehumig (Chronological Table);[4]

[1] Journal of the Asiatic Society of Bengal, N.S., Vol. L, Pt. I.
[2] *Ibid.*, 1887, Pt. I, pp. 1—307.
[3] *Ibid.*, 1888, Pt. I, pp. 41—48.
[4] *Ibid.*, 1889, Pt. I, pp. 37—84.

The marriage customs of Tibet;[1]

A note on the antiquity of Chittagong, compiled from the Tibetan works, Pagsam Jon-Zañ of Sumpa Khan-po, and Kāhbab Dun-dan of Lama Tārānātha;[2]

A note on the identity of the great Tsang-po of Tibet with the Dihong;[3]

The Hierarchy of the Dalai Lama[4] (1406—1745);

Tibet under the Tartar Emperors of China in the thirteenth century A.D;[5]

The Monasteries of Tibet;[6]

Life of Atisa.[7]

Lastly we must speak of his monumental Tibetan-English Dictionary, which was published by the Bengal Government in 1902. The origin of this Dictionary is as follows: As the result of his two journeys to Tibet and his residence there, Sarat Ch. Das brought with him four Tibetan Dictionaries. One of these was a

[1] Journal of the Asiatic Society of Bengal, 1893, Pt. III, pp. 8—33.

[2] *Ibid.*, 1898, Pt. I, pp. 20—28.

[3] *Ibid.*, 1898, pp. 126—129.

[4] *Ibid.*, 1904.

[5] *Ibid.*, 1904, pp. 94—102.

[6] *Ibid.*, 1905, pp. 106—116.

[7] *Ibid.*, 1891, pp. 46—53.

Tibetan-Sanskrit Dictionary of the thirteenth century A.D., and the other was a Sanskrit-Tibetan Dictionary compiled from the Buddhist Tantric books. In June, 1889, he was specially deputed by the Government of Bengal to compile a Tibetan-English Dictionary with the help of the four dictionaries brought from Tibet. It took him ten long years to finish that voluminous work (1899). It is interesting to note that his 'Dictionary' is the best ever published and has not been superseded by any other.

Dr. Laurence Austine Waddel, who was born on 29 May, 1854, devoted the best part of his life to the study of Tibetan Buddhism. His book 'The Buddhism of Tibet or Lamaism with its Mystic Cults, Symbolism and Mythology, and in its Relation to Indian Buddhism,' which was published in 1895, is still the standard work on the subject. Some of his important contributions are :

A Trilingual list of Nāga Rājās from the Tibetan;[1]

Buddha's secret, from a sixth century Pictorial Commentary and Tibetan Tradition;[2]

Description of Lhāsa Cathedral, translated from the Tibetan;[3]

A Historical Basis for the questions of King "Menander," from the Tibetan, etc.;[4]

Tibetan Folk Lore;[5]

Lamaism and its Sects;[6]

The motive of the mystery play of Tibet;[7]

A Tibetan Guide-book to the lost sites of the Buddha's Birth and Death;[8]

The French scholar M. Léon Feer wrote about the language and religion of Tibet in an article entitled—'Le Tibet, le Buddhisme et la Langue tibétaine' which appeared in "Revue Orientale et Américaine" (MDCCCLX,

[1] Journal of the Royal Asiatic Society, January, 1894, pp. 91—102.

[2] *Ibid.*, 1894, pp. 367—84.

[3] J. A. S. B., 1895, Pt. I, pp. 259—83.

[4] J. R. A. S., April, 1897, pp. 227—237.

[5] Indian Antiquary, 1892, p. 376, etc.

[6] Imp. & Asiat. Quart. Rev., 1894, N. S., VII, pp. 137—147.

[7] Actes Xe Cong. Int. Orient, 1894, 4^e part, pp. 167—172.

[8] J. A. S. B, 1896, Pt. I, pp. 275—279.

pp. 157—190). In the "Journal Asiatique" he published 'Le Karma-Jātaka' (1901). Before the seventh International Oriental Congress he read a paper on the 'Etymologie, Histoire, Orthographe du mot Tibet' (1886). He also published his 'Fragments, extraits du Kandjour traduits du tibétain,' in the "Annales du Musée Guimet".[1]

Lastly we shall speak of MM. Satish Ch. Vidyabhusan. He went to the Tibetan monasteries of Labrang and Phodang in Sikkim to consult the Tibetan Manuscripts there in May, 1907. Again in October, 1908, he visited Pamianychi, an old monastery in Tibet. His 'History of the Mediaeval School of Indian Logic,' (published in 1909) is very interesting. He edited "Nāyavindu" and "Amarkosa" in Tibetan for the Asiatic Society of Bengal. His important articles are :

History of the Mâdhyamika Philosophy of Nâgârjuna ;[2]

[1] V—pp. 1—557, 1883.

[2] Journal of the Pali Text Society, 1897, Pt. IV, pp. 7—20.

Indian Logic as preserved in Tibet;[1]

Lankāvatāra Sūtra;[2]

Dignāga and his Pramāna-Samuccaya;[3]

Sanskrit works on Literature, Grammar, Rhetoric and Lexicography as preserved in Tibet;[4]

A Tibetan Almanac for 1906—1907;[5]

On certain Tibetan scrolls and Images lately brought from Gyantse;[6]

Gyantse Rock Inscription of Choṣ-ṛgyal-gñis-pa, a ruler under the Sakyapa Hierarch in the fourteenth century A.D.[7]

What we know at present of Buddhism in Tibet and of the Indian pandits preaching in that land of Bhots is due to the researches of Western and Eastern scholars in this direction. Much still remains to be done.

---

[1] J. A. S. B., 1907.
[2] J. R. A. S., 1906.
[3] J. A. S. B., 1905.
[4] *Ibid.*, 1907.
[5] *Ibid.*, 1906, pp. 455—466.
[6] M. A. S. B., Vol. I, No. 1, pp. 1—23.
[7] J. A. S. B., 1906.

CHAPTER II

BUDDHIST UNIVERSITIES

WITH the foundation of the Pāla Empire in Eastern India a number of Universities grew up. The Pāla Kings were patrons of Buddhism, so they took special interest in creating new centres of culture, where Buddhist monks could busy themselves in cultivating the ancient learning of India. The monastery of Nālanda, which existed even before their time, came under their direct control. They used to appoint the abbots of that monastery. In the eighth century, Dharmapāla founded the monastery of Vikramasīlā. The Vihāra of Odantapuri was a little older. King Rama Pāla established the University of Jagaddala.

These were the centres of culture in Eastern India from the eighth to the twelfth century A.D. They produced a number of scholars like Padma Sambhava, Sânta Raksita, Dipamkara and others who went over to Tibet to preach Buddhism. These Vihāras brought India into touch with Tibet and her people. The monks of whom we shall speak wrote and translated many Buddhist books into Tibetan. Many of them were translated in the monasteries of Nālanda, Vikramasīlā and Jagaddala.

The story of Indian pandits going to China, Tibet and other countries is now almost forgotten. These Indian pandits served as agents for the spread of Indian civilisation and culture. They also brought India and Tibet into close contact. They were inspired with the universal idea of mankind as preached by Lord Buddha; and it was this inspiration which enabled them to bear all the hardships and difficulties of their way.

The introduction of Buddhism saw the advent of Indian missionaries in Tibet. It must be remembered that though Tibet was so near to India, though only the Himālayas separated the two countries, it took several centuries for Buddhism to penetrate into the country of Bhots (Tibet). Early in the first century China received Buddhism as one of her religions. Her example was followed by Corea in the fourth century A.D. In the sixth century A.D., Buddhist missionaries from Corea crossed over to Japan and introduced Buddhism in that Land of the Rising Sun. Thus while Buddhism had travelled from India to Gandhara, and from Gandhara to Chinese Turkistan and China, from China to Corea, and from Corea to Japan, Tibet, confined as she was by the mountains and seas, did not extend a happy welcome to the faith of Lord Buddha.

When Mahomet, the Prophet of Islam, was preaching his own religion in Arabia, a new movement had begun in the land of Bhots. With the reign of Sron-Tsan Gampo a new age dawned in Tibet. In his time the *Bon* religion was prevailing in his kingdom, but matrimonial alliances brought him into touch with the religion of Lord Buddha. In his battles for the extension of his dominions, the Tibetan monarch came into conflict with the Chinese king, Ch'itsung Luntsan, who was forced to make peace with him by giving his daughter, Wench'eng, a devout Buddhist, in marriage to him in A.D. 641.[1] This marital union was the turning-point in his life. The Chinese Princess influenced the Tibetan King to accept the creed of Lord Buddha. Soon afterwards he married Bhrikuti Devi, the daughter of Amsu Varman, the King of Nepal. At the time of his later marriage, Sron-Tsan Gampo promised the Nepalese King

[1] Dr. L. Austine Waddel, M.B.—*The Buddhism of Tibet or Lamaism.*

to try his best to introduce the Buddhist religion amongst the uncivilised Tibetans. He also promised to establish no less than five thousand monasteries throughout his kingdom. By their combined efforts these two Buddhist Princesses were soon able to convert the Tibetan King to the faith of the Buddha.[1]

Henceforward, he devoted his attention to the spread of Buddhism in Tibet. He sent out ambassadors to invite Buddhist monks from India, Nepal and China. The ambassador despatched to India, was named Thonmi Sam-Bhota (meaning, in sanskrit, *Sat-Bhota* or a good Tibetan, used as a sanskrit title). His real name was Thon-Mi, the son of Anu. It is not definitely known when he came to India, but some hold that he visited India in A.D. 632 and returned to Tibet in A.D. 650. The chinese traveller Yuan-Chwang also visited

[1] "Description of Lhāsa Cathedral"—L. A. Waddel in J. A. S. B., 1895, Pt. I, pp. 259—283.

India about this time. Thon-Mi passed some years in India learning Sanskrit under Lipi-Datta, a Brahman, and Deva-Vida Sinha. When he returned to Tibet, he took away many Buddhist manuscripts with him. It was he who introduced the Tibetan alphabet by modifying the Gupta characters a little. He used the new alphabet for the Grammar and other books, which he soon produced. At the invitation of the King, many Buddhist monks began to pour into Tibet. From India went Kusara ? (Kumāra) and Sankara Brahman, and from Nepal came Sila Manju. China and Kasmira also sent their quota.

Thus, the Buddhist Kings of Tibet found it necessary to invite the missionaries from India to propagate the Buddhist faith in their country. From the sixth century onward Indian pandits began to penetrate into that country either to preach or reform the Buddhist religion. Invited by the Tibetan Kings, Indian monks engaged themselves in translating Buddhist books from Sanskrit into the Tibetan language. It was the Indian monks with whom Tibetan Buddhist literature began to develop. Tibetan monks also began to learn Sanskrit under Indian monks and to translate Buddhist books into Tibetan.

Tibetan kings like Khri-Sroṅ-Lde-Btsan and Ralpachan invited many Indian pandits to preach Buddhism there. The *guru* of the former King was an Indian, Sānta Rakṣita by name. Following the advice of his *guru*, the king invited many celebrated Indian scholars like Padma Sambha. King Ralpachan also invited renowned monks like Pandita Jina Mitra and others.[1]

Where did these numerous Indian pandits come from? They came principally from the monasteries established in Bengal, Magadha and Kasmira. The monasteries of Nālanda,

[1] S. C. Das—"Contributions on Tibet". J. A. S. B., 1882.

Vikramasīlā, Jagaddala and Odantapuri, centres of culture for many centuries, supplied these pandits for Tibet. Tibetan and Sanskrit were there taught to Indian and Tibetan monks, and there also the translations of many Sanskrit books into Tibetan were made.

We shall take up these Universities one by one and sketch the lives of the Indian pandits who went up to Tibet from them, dealing first with the Vikramasīlā Vihāra, then with the Universities of Nālanda, Jagaddala and Odantapuri.

CHAPTER III

PANDITS OF VIKRAMASĪLA

THE University of Vikramasīlā was the centre from whence the largest number of Indian missionaries went to Tibet. From there learned pandits like Dipamkara Sri Jñāña, Abhyakara Gupta, Vairocana and others went to the court of the Tibetan King. Lama Tārānātha places the site of this University on a precipitous hill in Magadha on the bank of the Ganges.[1] General Cunningham identified it with Silāo, a small village near Bargāon in the district of Patna.[2] Mahāmahopādhyāya Satischandra Vidyābhusana placed it in the Bhagalpur District.[3] Mr. N. Dey in his article on " The

[1] Tārānātha's "*Geschichte des Buddhismus,*" pp. 234—242.

[2] Archæological Report, Vol. VIII, p. 83.

[3] Indian Logic : Mediæval School, p. 150.

Vikramasīlā Monastery" settled the question of identification by placing it at Pātharghātā, near Colgong, in the district of Bhagalpur.[1] The ancient name of Pātharghātā was Vikramasīlā-Sanghārāma, or in its abbreviated form Sīlā-Sangama—the monastery of Vikramasīlā.

This University of Vikramasīlā was founded by King Dharmapāla in the eighth century A.D. From the time of its foundation it began to send pandits to Tibet. Some of the pandits of this University were:

Buddha Jñāñapāda; Vairocana Raksita; Jetāri; Prajnā Karamati; Vāgisvara Kirti; Ratna-Vajra; Jñāña-Sri-Mitra; Ratnākara Sānti; Virya Simha; Dipamkara Sri-Jnāna (Atisa); Abhayakara Gupta; Tathāgata Raksita; and Dharma Kirti.

(1.)

Ācārya Buddha Jñāñapāda

One of the earliest pandits of the Vikramasīlā Vihāra was Acārya Buddha Jñāñapāda.

[1] J. A. S. B., 1909, Jan.

Lāmā Tārānātha speaks of him in his History of Buddhism.[1] He was associated with this University in the early stages of its development. He was the King Dharmapāla who founded Sri Vikramasīlā Vihāra,[2] which Tārānātha places on a hillock on the bank of the Ganges in Northern Magadha. He also gives an elaborate description of the whole monastery. The founder took every care to make it an ideal Vihāra in every sense of the word. There was in the centre the temple with Mahābodhi images. Within the enclosure fifty-three smaller temples of private character and fifty-four ordinary temples were set up. Thus the total number of temples within the compound of the monastery was one hundred and eight. It was surrounded with a strong wall. King Dharmapāla not only endowed the University in this way, but

[1] Schiefner's *Tāranātha*, p. 220.

[2] *Ibid.*, p. 217.

also made ample provision for the accommodation of professors and students. He also realised that temples and hostels alone would not make the new Vihāra a centre of culture for the whole of India. Something more was needed—professors. Accordingly he made provision for no less than one hundred and eight pandits, also for :—a wood-offering (*streu opfer*) ācārya, an ordination ācārya, a fire-offering (*brand-opfer*) ācārya, a superintendent of works (*bya-ba-bsruṇ-ba*), a guard of pigeons, and a supplier of temple servants.

Thus Dharmapāla provided for no less than one hundred and fourteen learned men in his new University. They received from the royal treasury their necessaries, their food and clothing. It may be mentioned that the cost of the maintenance of one of them was ordinarily equivalent to that of four men.

There was a strong board of eminent professors to conduct the teaching of this

University. Lama Tārānātha makes an interesting comment in this connection. He remarks that this board of professors kept watch over the affairs of the Nālandā Vihāra[1] also. If we accept his statement, it must be admitted that a spirit of co-operation prevailed between these two sister Universities. Both were directly under King Dharmapāla, who may have asked the board of the new University to watch over the older University. Sometimes we find men like Dīpamkara and Abhayakara Gupta working in both Universities. We, however, do not know whether the Nālandā University was conducted under the direction of the pandits of Vikramasīlā. What Tārānātha says is this: "*Der Vorstand dieser Lehrstätte hütette auch Nālandā.*"

On the authority of Tārānātha, we learn that our monk was living at the same time as

[1] Schiefner's *Tārānātha*, p. 218.

King Dharmapāla and the Tibetan King, Khri Sron lde Btsan, who were contemporaries. In his time lived the following pandits:

Kaljāṇa Gupta; Simhabhadra; Cobhavjuha; Sāgara Megha; Prabhākara; Pūrṇa Vardhana; Buddha Jñāñapāda; Buddha Guhja; Buddha Sānti; Ācārya Padmākaraghosa of Kasmira; Dharmākara Datta; and Simha-mukha.

It is interesting to note that our monk, Buddha Jñāñapāda, was among these pandits famous for their learning. He was the prominent disciple of Simhabhadra, living in the time of Dharmapāla. After the death of his *guru*, Simhabhadra, Ācārya Buddha Jñāñapāda was appointed the royal priest, perhaps of King Dharmapāla. Not long after, he was engaged as the Ordination Priest of Vikramasīlā. Thus he was brought into close touch with the Vikramasīlā Vihāra. Afterwards he was drawn to the cult of *Vadschrātschārja* (Vajrācārya) in the same University. From its foundation this Vihāra developed as a great centre of *Mantra-Vajrācarya*, and Buddha Jñāñapāda was one of the great propounders of this cult.

Our monk, who flourished in the eighth century A.D., was a follower of Tantricism. He composed several books on Tantra. In the catalogue of Tibetan Tripitaka, we find the following nine books compiled by him (they are translated into Tibetan by several hands):

'Mukhāgama';[1]
'Samanta-shadra-nāma-sādhana';[2]
'Sri hêruka-sadhana';[3]
'Āṭma sādhanāvatāra-nāma';[4]
'Bhattārakārya-jambhala-jalêndra-sādhana.'[5]
'Guhya-jambhala-sādhana.'[6]
'Vistara-jambhala-sādhana.'[6]
'Gati-vyuha.'[6]

1 Catalogue of Tibetan Tripitaka, II, p. 147.
2 *Ibid.*
3 *Ibid.*
4 *Ibid.*, II, p. 148.
5 *Catalogue du Fond tibétain* par P. Cordier, II, p. 148.
6 *Ibid.*

'Samanta-bhadrārtha-samgraha.'[1]

There are three other books, which appear under the name of Buddha Sri Jñāñapāda, who was perhaps no other than the great pandit Buddha Jñāñapāda. They are:

'Dwi-krama-tatwa-bhāvanā nāma āmukhādhyā pana.'[2]
'Caturaṇga-sādhanopāyikā Samantabhadra-nāma.'[3]
'Mukti-tilaka-namā.'[4]

Unfortunately the Sanskrit versions of these books are lost to us, only the Tibetan translations exist. We are not in a position to state definitely whether he visited Tibet or not. We bring in the sketch of his life only because he prepared the ground for the future pandits of the University of Vikramasīlā.

[1] *Catalogue du Fond tibétain*, par P. Cordier, II, p. 152.

[2] *Ibid.*, p. 146.

[3] *Ibid.*, p. 147.

[4] *Ibid.*

(2.)

VAIROCANA RAKṢITA

Vairocana Rakṣita was one of the monks of the University of Vikramasīlā, who went to Tibet to propagate Buddhism. It is unfortunate that we do not know much about this monk. In Tibetan books he is known as 'Dpal Rnam-par Snaṅ-mdsad Sruṅ-ba' (Sri Vairocana Rakṣita). He bore the well-known title of 'Mahāpandita' as well as that of 'Mahācārya'. He was proficient in Tibetan, and translated some of his own Sanskritic Buddhist works into that language. Vikramasīlā was the place chosen for the composition as well as the translation of his own books. He wrote the following two books in Sanskrit and also translated them into Tibetan :

'Sri-vajra-bhaîrava-sādhana-vajra-prakāsa-nāma.'[1]

[1] *Catalogue du Fond tibétain* par P. Cordier, II, p. 175.

'Sri-vajra-bhaîrava-maṇḍala-vidhi-prakāsa-nāma.'[1]

From an incidental reference in one of his books, we come to know that our monk Vairocana Rakṣita was the son of He-ḥddod of Spa-gor or Pa-gor. We are, however, in the dark as to the particulars of his father. It is difficult also to identify the native place of this monk. The same source informs us that he was the disciple of Padma Sambhava and the contemporary of the Tibetan King, Khri Sron lde Btsan.[2]

Now, who was this Khri Sron lde Btsan? He was one of the celebrated Kings of Tibet. He was born, according to Tibetan history, in A.D. 728 and died in A.D. 864. He invited to his court many Indian pandits, such as Santa Rakṣita, Padma-Sambhava and others (A.D. 749). He was a

[1] *Catalogue du Fond tibétain* par P. Cordier, II, p. 175

[2] *Ibid.*, III, p. 521.

zealous patron of Buddhism, and constructed the great monastery of Sam-ye (A.D. 749) after the model of the Odantapura Vihāra of Magadha.[1] Vairocana Rakṣita, according to the Tibetan sources, was the contemporary of Khri Sron lde Btsan, and therefore must have flourished somewhere between A.D. 728 and A.D. 864. His *guru*, Padma Sambhava, went to Tibet to propagate Buddhism in A.D. 749. Vairocana Rakṣita must, therefore, have received instructions from his *guru* before Padma Sambhava's departure for Tibet. Vairocana at that time, might have been twenty years old; so we can assert that he flourished in the second quarter of the eighth century A.D.

After finishing his education under Padma Sambhava, he perhaps joined the University of Vikramasīlā and engaged himself mainly in

[1] S. C. Das—J. A. S. B., 1882, p. 2, and Vidyabhusan's *Indian Logic: Mediæval School*, pp. 124—5.

composing Buddhist books into Sanskrit and translating some of them into Tibetan.

Following in the foot-steps of his *guru*, he may have gone to Tibet. Two of his works 'Mantra-Vivṛṭa-prajñā-hrdaya-vrtti' and 'Ratna-vāda-cakra'[1]—were composed mainly for the Tibetan King, Khri Sron lde Btsan, to whom he explained the contents. It was necessary for him to go over to the country of Bhots to propound the doctrines of Lord Buddha to the Tibetan King, and for that purpose he had collected the materials of his first book from the well-known Prajnā-pāramitā-hṛdaya-sūtra. It seems evident then that Vairocana Rakṣita visited Tibet to propagate the faith of Lord Buddha during the reign of Khri Sron lde Btsan. He might have come after the advent of his *guru*, Padma Sambhava, and of Sānta Rakṣita (A.D. 749).

Mahāpandita Vairocana Rakṣita composed the following eight books in Sanskrit, which

[1] *Catalogue du Fond tibétain*, III, p. 490.

were rendered into Tibetan by various scholars:

'Rakṭa-yamāri-sādhana.'[1]
'Bodhisattva-caryāvatāra-pañjikā.'[2]
'Sikṣā-kusuma-mañjari-nāma.'[3]
'Siṣya-līkha-ṭippaṇa.'[4]
'Commentary of Mūla Tantra.'[5]
'The Essence of Doctrines.'[6]
'Mantra-vivṛṭa-prajña-hṛdaya-vṛtti.'[7]
'Ratna-vāda-cakra.'[8]

As Vairocana Rakṣita was a profound Tibetan scholar, he translated the following Tāntric and other works into that language:

'Mahā-gaṇapati-dhātu-Trikara-Rakta-Vaṣi-kara-Sādhana.'[9]

[1] *Catalogue du Fond tibétain*, II, p. 179.
[2] *Ibid.*, III, p. 308.
[3] ,, p. 326.
[4] ,, p. 430.
[5] ,, p. 521.
[6] ,, p. 521.
[7] ,, p. 489.
[8] ,, p. 490.
[9] ,, p. 221.

'Gaṇapati-samaya-guhya-sādhana-nāma.'[1]
'Hêruka-pañca-sādhana-nāma.'[2]
'Phala-jñānêka-bhumi-dharma-dhātu.'[3]
'Pāramita-samāsa-nāma.'[4]
'Vinaya-samgraha.'[5]
'Sukla-vajra-yoginī-sādhana.'[6]
'Kalpa-saptaka-vṛtti.'[7]
'Mahêsānanasya-sādhana.'[7]
'Prajñā-pāramitā-hṛdaya-sādhana.'[8]

Here also the originals are lost, only the Tibetan versions are now existing.

Our monk should not be confused either with Vairocana, the interpreter-monk who translated 'Nyāyāloka-siddhi' into Tibetan[9] or

[1] *Catalogue du Fond tibétain*, III, p. 229.

[2] *Ibid.*, p. 229.

[3] „ p. 237.

[4] „ p. 326.

[5] „ p. 401. (This translation was only corrected by him.)

[6] *Ibid.*, II, p. 55.

[7] „ p. 169.

[8] „ p. 286.

[9] S. C. Vidyabhusan's *Indian Logic: Mediæval School*, p. 123.

with Sri Vairocana Vajra, a native of Kosala, who translated 'Dohākosa' into Tibetan.

(3.)

JETĀRI

Ācārya Jetāri was one of the prominent graduates of the Vikramasīlā Vihāra. He influenced Tibetan thought to a considerable degree and all his books on Tantra and Sutra were translated into Tibetan. His life has been preserved by Lama Tārānātha in his 'History of Buddhism'.[1] Tārānātha informs us that Ācārya Jetāri hailed from Varendra (Northern Bengal). His Father, Garbhapāda, was living at the court of King Sanātana, a vassal of the Pāla Kings of Bengal. Garbhapāda, an ācārya of the Brahmana caste, ordained King Sanātana and obtained many gifts from him. When Jetāri became seven

[1] A. Schiefner's *Tārānātha*, p. 230; Vidyabhusan's *Logic*, p. 136.

years old, he was sent to the school to learn the sciences and in a few years he became proficient in various branches, specially in Abhidharma. Soon after Jetāri became an *Upāsaka* and learned from his father the doctrines of *Guhjasamadscha*, *Sambara* and *Hevadschra*. His father died when King Mahapāla was reigning over Bengal. At that time Jetāri was not yet the proud recipient of a diploma, but during the reign of King Mahápāla (A.D. 899—940 according to the Tibetan authorities) he received the royal diploma of Pandita of the Vikramasīlā-Vihāra from the hands of the king himself.

Jetāri remained at the Vikramasīlā University as a professor. It was from him that Ratnākara Sānti learned the texts of Sutra and Tantra at Vikramasīlā. Ratnākara Sānti was appointed a gate-keeper in the same Vihāra about A.D. 983. The reputed reformer, Dipamkara or Atisa, born in A.D. 980, was also trained by him in the five minor sciences. It can, therefore, be remarked that Jetāri flourished in the early part of the tenth century A.D.

By his numerous books, which were available to the Tibetans through translations, he influenced the thought and culture of their country. Tārānātha informs us that Pandit Jetāri produced one hundred books, including Tantras and Sutras. Unfortunately, we find only twenty-two books of his preserved in their Tibetan versions. He may not have been a Tibetan scholar, as no Tibetan translation by him is known to us. His books were so popular among Buddhists that they were eagerly translated into Tibetan by various monks. Nine of his books on Tantra are the following:

'Hêvajrasya-sêkanischaya-nāma.'[1]

'Sri-dasa-krodha-vidyā-vidhi-nāma.'[1]

[1] *Catalogue du Fond tibétain*, II, p. 84.

'Sri-catuha-pîṭa-tatwa-catuska.'[1]
'Nāthakṣobhya-sādhana.'[2]
'Arya-lokêsvara-cintâmani-cakravarti-sādhana.'[3]
'Sîta-vaṭî-sādhana.'[4]
'Mahāprati-sarācakra-lêkhana-vidhi.'[5]
'Māyā-jāla-kramāvalokitêsvara-sādhana.'[6]
'Catura-mudrā-sādhana-nāma.'[7]

Jetāri probably was also the author of the following five Tantras:

'Pratisara-sādhana.'[8]
'Ārya-mahā-māyurî-sādhana.'[8]
'Mahā-sahasra-pramardanî-sādhana.'[8]
'Ārya-mahā-mantrānudhāraṇî-sādhana.'[8]
'Paṇca-rakṣārcana-vidhi.'[9]

[1] *Catalogue du Fond tibétain*, II, p. 101.
[2] *Ibid.*, p. 289.
[3] " p. 319.
[4] " p. 366.
[5] " p. 367.
[6] *Ibid.*, III, p. 20.
[7] " p. 123.
[8] *Ibid*, II, p. 366.
[9] " p. 367.

His works on Sutra (*Mdo-Hgrel*) are the following eight:

'Bodhi-cittotpāda-samādāna-vidhi.'[1]
'Suṭamaṭa-vibhaṇga-kārikā.'[2]
'Bodhyāpaṭṭidesanā-vṛitti Bodhi-sattvā-siksā-krama nāma.'[3]
'Hêtu-tattvapadêṣa.'[4]
'Dharma-dharmi-viniscḥaya.'[5]
'Bālāvatāra-tarka-nāma.'[6]
'Sugaṭa-maṭa-vibhanga-kārika.'[7]
'Sugaṭa-maṭa-vibhanga-bhāṣya.'[8]

(4.)

PRAJÑĀKARAMATI

Prajñākaramati was one of the great pandits and gate-keepers of Vikramasīlā Vihāra. As

[1] *Catalogue du Fond tibétain*, III, p. 332.
[2] *Ibid.*, p. 356.
[3] ,, p. 368.
[4] ,, p. 454. (See Vidyabhusan's Logic, pp. 136--137.)
[5] ,, ,, (,, ,, ,,)
[6] ,, p. 455. (,, ,, ,,)
[7] ,, p. 496.
[8] *Ibid.*

is well-known there were six gates in this Vihāra. These gates were presided over by great scholars, who used to test the knowledge of the students coming to prosecute their studies in the University. If they failed in the test examination, they were not allowed to join the Uuniversity. Our monk Prajñākaraınati presided over the Southern gate. At that time, according to Tārānatha, the six guardians were:

Prajñākaramati, of the Southern gate; Ratnākara Sānti, of the Eastern gate; Vāgisvara Kirti, of the Western gate; Naropa, of the Northern gate; Ratna Vajra, of the first Central gate; Jñāña Sri Mitra, of the second Central gate.

Prajñākaramati was a great scholar and learned in all the sciences. Once he entered into a hot discussion with a Tirthaja but before the discussion began he offered sacrifice to image of Manjusri and prayed devotedly to him. By the grace of Manjusri he easily understood all the questions put to him by Tirthaja, and defeated his opponent in a short time.

As our monk was sometimes known by the name of Prajñākara, great confusion arose in connection with these two names—Prajñākaramati and Prajñākaragupta. Lama Tārānatha reminds us that there were two distinct personalities. One—our monk Prajñākaramati—was a *bhikshu* by profession, while the other, Prajñākaragupta, was only an *upāsaka*. They also flourished in different periods. Prajñāgupta lived during the reign of Mahā-Pāla, who died in A.D. 940;[1] while our monk, Prajñākaramati, appeared during the reign of King Canaka (A.D. 955—983).[2]

The influence of this monk on Tibetan thought was not very great. Only two books

[1] Vidyabhusan's *Logic*, p. 135.

[2] Tārānātha's *History of Buddhism*, p. 135.

are ascribed to him in the whole of the Tibetan Tripitaka collection. He composed one work on sutra, *Mdo-Hgrel*, in Sanskrit, namely, 'Abhisamayālaṁkara Vṛttipiṇḍārtha.'[1] Another book of his was 'Bodhicaryāvatāra Pañjikā'.[2] Both of these were popular and were translated by Mahapandita Sumati-Kirti.

Prajñākaramati was known to the Tibetans as 'Çes-ral hbyuṅ-gnas blogros'. He bore the title of Sri Mahāpandita. He was also called 'Aparadvārakapātapa' (or in Tibetan 'Nub-kyi sgo-glegs-pa'), which M. P. Cordier translates as "gardien de la porte occidentale, du monastère de Vikramasīlā" (guardian of the Western gate of the monastery of Vikramasīlā).[3] Lama Tārānātha, however, makes him the guardian of the Southern gate.[4] We are rather inclined to accept the view of Tārānātha.

[1] P. Cordier, *Catalogue du Fond tibétain*, III, p. 279.
[2] *Ibid.*, p. 306.
[3] ,, p. 279.
[4] *Tārānātha's Geschichte des Buddhismus*, von Schiefner, pp. 234, 235, etc.

(5.)

ĀCĀRYA RATNĀKARA SĀNTI

Ācārya Ratnākara Sānti was a great writer on Buddhism. His books reached the Tibetan Buddhists as translations. He was the contemporary of the monk Prajñākaramati, and presided over the Eastern gate of the Vikramasīlā monastery. Ratnākara Sāntī was known to the Tibetans as Ācārya Sānti—or Sānti-pa. In his early years, he was associated with the Odantapura University, where he received ordination in the school of Sarvāstivāda. Ratnākara Sānti afterwards joined the Vikramasīlā University, where he was taught the Tantra and Sutra texts by Ācārya Jetāri, Ratnakirti and others.

When did Ratnākara Sānti flourish? He was a gate-keeper of Vikramasīlā during the reign of King Canaka (A.D. 955—983). Jetāri his *guru* lived in the time of King Mahā

Pāla, who reigned up till A.D. 940. According to the Tibetan records Mahā Pāla was succeeded by Sāmu Pāla (A.D. 940—952), who was followed by Sresṭha Pāla or Praistha Pāla (952—955). Then came King Canaka to the throne (A.D. 955—983). As Acārya Ratnākara Sānti read under Ācārya Jetāri, he would be quite a young man in A.D. 940. Assuming that he was twenty-five years old in that year, we can assert that he was born about A.D. 915, thus, therefore, fixing his date as approximately A.D. 915—983.

Ratnākara Sānti bore the title of Mahāpandita. He was sometimes called Mahācārya or simply Ācārya. To the Tibetans he was known by the name of 'Rin-chen ḥlyuṅ-gnas shi-pa.' Invited by the King of Ceylon, he paid a visit to the southern island to propagate the Buddhist faith. We do not know whether he went to Tibet, but his religious writings were eagerly sought by the

Buddhists there, who translated all his books into Tibetan. The following thirteen books were written by him in Sanskrit:

'Svasmā-nāma-tīkā.'[1]
'Sri-hêvajra pañjikā muktikāvali nāma.'[2]
'Bhrama-hara-nāma-sādhana.'[3]
'Pindi-kṛta-sādhanopāyikā vṛtti ratnāvali nāma.'[4]
'Kusumaṇjali-nāma Gūhya-samāja-nivandha.'[5]
'A continuation of the preceding one.'[6]
'Sri-gūhya-samāja-mandala-vidhi-tikā.'[7]
'Sri-Kṛṣṇa-yamāri-mahā-Tantra Rāja-pañjikā ratna-pradipa-nâma.'[8]
'Kṛsṇa-yamāri-sādhana-praphulla-kumuḍa nāma.'[9]

[1] *Catalogue du Fond tibétain*, II, p. 32.
[2] *Ibid.*, II, p. 69.
[3] „ p. 80.
[4] „ p. 140.
[5] „ p. 145
[6] „ p. 146.
[7] „ p. 150.
[8] „ p. 159.
[9] „ p. 162.

'Vajra-bhaîrava-gaṇa-cakra-nāma.'[1]

'Sukha-dukkha-dvaya-parityāga-dṛsthi-nāma.'[2]

'Abhisêka-nirukṭi.'[3]

'Sri-sarva-rahasya-nibandha Rahasya-pra-dipa-nāma.'[4]

(6.)

JÑĀÑA SRI MITRA

Another gate-keeper of the University of Vikramasīlā was Mahāpandita Jñāña Sri Mitra. Lama Tārānātha speaks of him in his 'History of Indian Buddhism'.[5] He was the guardian of the second Central gate of the Vikramasīlā Vihāra. His native country was Gaṇḍa. MM. S. C. Vidyabhusana holds that Jñāña Sri and Jñāña Sri Mitra are the same. He goes further and says that probably he was

[1] *Catalogue du Fond tibétain*, II, p. 171.
[2] *Ibid.*, II, p. 235.
[3] ,, p. 253.
[4] ,, p. 282.
[5] Schiefner's *Tārānātha*, pp. 235—242.

also the same person as Jñāña Sri Bhadra, who worked in Kasmira.[1]

Jñāña Sri Mitra first belonged to the Srāvaka School of Buddhism, but afterwards changed his creed and joined the Mahāyāna school. He was the contemporary of Ratnavajra, Ratnākara Sānti and other gate-keepers of the time of King Canaka. He is said to have greatly assisted the famous Buddhist reformer Dipamkara Sri Jñāña (who was born in A.D. 980) in his early days. Our monk, therefore, seems to have flourished in the latter half of the tenth century A.D.

Jñāña Sri Mitra's name in Tibetan was 'Yeçes dpal bçes-gñen'. To spread the genius of India in Tibet, he learned Tibetan and translated one of his books, 'Pramāṇa-viniscaya-tîkā,' into Tibetan. Thus we know he was anxious to propagate the Buddhist doctrines in Tibet through translations.

[1] Vidyabhusan's *Indian Logic*, p. 137.

He composed other books on Buddhism in Sanskrit. Four of them are :

'Pramāna-viniscaya-tīkā.'[1]
'Kārya-kāraṇa-bhāva-siḍḍhi.'
'Tarka-bhāsā.'
'Vṛtta-mālā-stuti.'[2]

The first three of these are books on logic. There is another book called 'Sahaja-mandala-trayāloka-samjaṅāṅa-nāma,' which appears under the name of Mahāpandita Jñāña Sri. All these books were translated into Tibetan by various Tibetan Buddhist monks.

(7.)

Ratna Vajra

Upādhyāya Ratna Vajra, another gate-keeper pandit of Vikramasīlā, was the contemporary of Prajñākaramati, Ratnākara Sānti and others. Lama Tārānātha speaks of

[1] It was the commentary of *Prumāṇa-Viniscaya* by Dharmakirti.
[2] *Catalogue du Fond tibétain*, III, p. 467.

Ratnavajra as the keeper of the Middle gate of Vikramasīlā Vihāra.[1] He belonged to a Brahmana family of Kashmira. Formerly, there was a Brahmana named Mahesvara in whose family it was predicted that many famous wise men would be born. One such learned man of his family was the Brahmana Haribhadra, known as a celebrated pandit. Another was our monk Ratnavajra, his son. It must be said to the credit of Haribhadra that he was the first convert to Buddhism in his family. Ratnavajra was, accordingly, brought up in the Buddhist faith from his earliest years. He became an *upāsaka* in his youth. He remained in his native country, Kashmira, up to his thirty-sixth year, and studied, not only the sutras and mantras of the Buddhist literature, but most of the Buddhist sciences. Then he came to Magadha and visited the sacred Vajrāsana (Buddha-Gayā), where he saw

[1] A. Schiefner's *Tārānātha*, p. 240.

various Buddhist gods like Sakra-Saṁvara, Vajravarāhī and others. In a very short time he mastered all the Buddhist sāstras by the grace of these gods. Thence he came to further his studies in the Vikramasīlā Vihāra. After he finished the course of study in the University, the royal diploma of pandita was given to him by the King. Soon after he was appointed as the keeper of the Middle gate by King Canaka; and was a contemporary of Prajñākaramati and Ratnākara Sānti.

Ratnavajra was a great preacher of Buddhism. After occupying the post of gatekeeper for some time with credit, he went back to Kashmira, where he entered into a discussion with many Tirthajas, defeated them, and converted them to the faith of the Buddha. He was a tireless worker. From Kashmira, he went to the country of Uddyana, whence towards the end of his career he visited Tibet to spread the Buddhist faith. He passed the remainder of his life in preaching the Buddhist doctrines. While in Tibet, he learned the language and translated many Buddhist works into Tibetan. For the propagation of Buddhism, he became known to the Tibetans as Ācārya Ratna Vajra. He also bore the title of Māhā-pandita. His name in Tibetan was Siddhā-cārya Rin-chen rdo-rje, (Ratna Vajra) of Kasmira.

He was the author of the following fourteen Buddhistic books in Sanskrit, which found their way to Tibet through translations:

'Sri-hêruka-sȃdhana-nāma."[1]
'Sri-cakra-saṁbara-maṇḍala-maṇgala-gāthā.'[2]
'Sri-cakra-saṁbara-sṭoṭra.'[3]
'Bali-karma nāma.'[4]
'Sri-hêvajra-sṭoṭra.'[5]

[1] *Catalogue du Fond tibétain*, II, p. 43.
[2] *Ibid.*, p 43.
[3] „ p. 52.
[4] „ p. 89.
[5] „ p. 90.

'Mahā-māya-sādhana.'[1]

'Sri-sarva-Buddha-Samayoga-dākinī-jāla-sambara-mahā-tantra-raja-nāma-maṇḍalopāyikā Sarva-sattva-sukhodayā-nāma.'[2]

'Sri-akṣobhya-vajra-sādhana.'[3]

'Sri-cakra-saṁbara-maṇḍala-dêva-gaṇa-sṭoṭra-nāma.'[4]

'Mantra-rāja-samaya-siddhi-sādhana-nāma.'[5]

'Sri-cakra-saṁbarādwaya-vîra-sādhana.'[6]

'Arya-jambhala-sṭoṭra-nāma.'[7]

'Mahā-sênāpati-caturmūkha-sṭoṭra sloka-vimsaka nāma.'[8]

'Mêghāloka-gaṇapati-sādhana-nāma.'[9]

When in Tibet, Ratnavajra learned Tibetan and translated several books into that language.

[1] *Catalogue du Fond tibétan*, II, p. 103.
[2] *Ibid.*, p. 1[illegible]2.
[3] „ p. 153.
[4] „ p. 52.
[5] *Ibid.*, III, p. 219.
[6] „ p. 262.
[7] „ p. 223.
[8] „ p. 200.
[9] „ p. 88.

As a translator of Tibetan, he was sometimes known as Upādhyāya Ratna Vajra. Four of his translations are :

'Guhya-vajra-tantra-rāja-vṛtti.'[1]
'Gîti-tattwa-nāma.'[2]
'Abhisamaya-krama nāma.'[3]
'Sri-Ananda-puspa-mālā.'[4]

Ratnavajra was thus one of the earliest Indian pandits who went to Tibet to preach the genius of India and to develop the Buddhist literature of Tibet.

(8.)

Vāgisvara Kirti

The last of the famous gate-keepers of the University of Vikramasīlā was Vāgisvara Kirti. He hailed from Benares and in the reign of King Canaka (A.D. 955—983). He was appointed as the keeper of the Western gate

[1] *Catalogue du Fond tibétain*, II, p. 30.
[2] *Ibid.*, p. 73.
[3] „ p. 74.
[4] „ p. 97.

of the Vikāra ; and was the contemporary of the pandits Prajñākaramati, Ratnākara Sànti, Ratna-vajra and others. He bore both the titles of Ācārya and Mahā pandita. He was a follower of Tārā Devî (' Lha-mo Sgrol-ma ').

He was not a great writer. He wrote only one book on Tantra, entitled, ' Mṛtyu-bañcanopadesa,' of which the composition was due to the inspiration he received from Tārā Dêvî. It also found its way to the Tibetan public through the translation of Upādhāya Dipaṁkara Sri Jñāña of India, who was assisted by the monk Ratnabhadra.[1] The Sanskrit version is lost, the Tibetan version only is existing. The latter contains three sets of diagrams.

His name in Tibetan was Ṅag-gi dbaṅ-phyug grags-pa. MM. Satis Chandra Vidyābhusan says that perhaps Vāgisvara Kirti was the same as Vāk-Praja.[2]

[1] *Vide* Cordier—*Catalogue du Fond tibétain*, II, p. 167.

[2] S. C. Vidyabhusan's *Indian Logic*, p. 141.

(9.)

DIPAṀKARA SRI JṄĀṄA

The greatest of the Buddhist missionaries going from India across the lofty Himālayas was Dipaṁkara Sri Jṅāṅa, who was also known as Upādhāya Atisa. At the call of the Buddhist King of Tibet, Chaṅ Chûb, he left the Monastery of Vikramasīlā and went to Tibet to reform the Buddhist religion in the country of the Bhots.[1]

Upādhāya Dipaṁkara Sri Jṅāṅa was descended from the royal family of Ganḍa, a kingdom to the east of Vajrāsana (Gaya). Born in A.D. 980 he received special training from the sage Jetāri. His father was Kalyāna Sri (Ḍge-vaḥī ḍpal) and his mother was Prabhâvati. His parents christened him Chandragarbha. He soon became proficient not only in the Mahāyāna

[1] S. C. Das—*Indian Pandits in the Land of Snow* (1893), pp. 50—76. Waddell—*Lamaism.*

and Hīnayāna doctrines, but also in the Vaiseshika philosophy, and especially in the Tantras.

Though he came from the royal family of Gaṇḍa he, like Lord Buddha, renounced the ease and pleasure of the world and entered the monastery of Krshṇagiri, where he was trained by Rahula Gupta. There he received the new name of Guhya-jñāṅa Vajra. When he was nineteen years old, he took the sacred vows according to Buddhist Law, from Sila Rakshita, who was the Mahā Sānghika Ācārya of Odantapuri. From him, he received the name Dipaṁkara Sri Jñāṅa, by which he became generally known to the Buddhists of India and of Tibet. When he was thirty-one years old, he was ordained by Acārya Dharma Raksita in the highest order of Bhikshus.

Thus completing his education in India, he sailed off to Suvarnadvipa (identified by

S. C. Das with Sudharmanagar in Pegu, now called Thaton) which was considered the head-quarters of Buddhism in the East. He learned all the mysteries of Buddhism from Ācārya Chandrakirti, the High Priest of Suvarnadvipa. After residing there for twelve years, Dipaṁkara returned to India, visiting Ceylon on his way home. He was associated with such learned men of the time as Sānti, Naropānta, Kusala and others. Dipaṁkara soon became famous for his deep knowledge of the mysteries of Buddhism. He defeated many Tirthaka heretics in a discussion at Vajrāsana (Buddha Gaya); and was soon promoted as the head of the community of Buddhist monks at Magadha and Ganḍa. King Naya Pāla was then ruling over the destinies of Bengal and Magadha (from 1030). He was attracted by the versatility of this great Buddhist scholar and appointed him to the post of High Priest of Vikramasīlā.

About this time the Tibetan King, Chañ Chūb, wanted to invite a great Indian pandit to reform the Buddhism of Tibet, which had become a little corrupted as time passed. He told his ministers: "Religious service on a grand scale should be performed at Lhāsa and Samyé, and a great Pandita, holy and learned, should be brought here from India." Accordingly a worthy envoy, Tshul Khrim-gyalwa of the Nag-tcho family, was selected to proceed to India. He had already been there to study Sanskrit. He was a learned Lochâva (Sanskrit interpreter) and translated a few Sanskrit books into Tibetan. The story of this embassy has been well narrated by Rai Bahadur Sarat Ch. Das from Tibetan sources. The account of the journey, how they overcame the numerous dangers and difficulties of the way, reads almost like a romance. The majestic religious assembly witnessed by the envoys at Vikramasīlā leaves a profound impression on the mind of the reader. When requested by the Tibetan envoy to proceed to Tibet at the invitation of the King, Dipaṁkara replied: "I have now grown advanced in age and have the keys of many monasteries in my charge and many works still remain unfinished, so I cannot shortly set out for Tibet."

Afterwards Dipaṁkara invoked the advice of the Goddess Tārā, who informed him of the good he could render to Tibet by going over there, but at the cost of shortening his life by twenty years. Thereupon he determined to go with the Tibetan embassy. The pandits of the Vikramasīlā Vihāra, Ratna Kirti, Vairochana Raksita, Kanaka-sri of Nepal and others, very unwillingly parted from him. He started with pandit Bhūmi Garbha, Nag-tcho, Gya-tson, Bhūmi Saṅgha, Virya Chandra and others, who went with him as far as Mitra Vihāra. When the great pandit

Dipaṁkara reached Tibet all the people "sang a song of welcome like those wise ministers of King Thi-Sroṅ-deu-tsan, who three centuries ago had escorted ācārya Sānta Rakshita from the confines of India to Tibet". An escort of three hundred horsemen took the sage to the Tibetan King, who welcomed him warmly, and surnamed him Jovo Je[1] as he was the wisest pandit of India. He commanded his subjects to receive the teachings of Lord Buddha from the Indian Sage and Dipaṁkara began to preach among them. He rescued Tibetan Buddhism from the gross corruption into which it was fast sinking by reforming it. Although he might be called the real founder of Lamaism, he did not assume the title of Lama (or Guru) even when he was the head of the Buddhist monks in Tibet. It was his disciple Brom-ton, who after his death became the founder of the first great

[1] Sans. Prabhu Svāmi.

hierarchy of Tibet. After preaching the doctrines of Lord Buddha throughout Tibet for a period of thirteen years (A.D. 1040—1053) ācārya Dipaṁkara breathed his last at Nethan, near Lhāsa, at the age of seventy-three (A.D. 1053).

The influence exercised by Dipaṁkara on Tibetan thought and culture cannot be overestimated: he gave a fresh lease of life to Tibetan Buddhism. By means of his numerous books, all of which were translated into Tibetan, his theories were propagated.

Dipaṁkara was a great Tibetan scholar as well. He was perhaps the greatest writer of Tibetan Buddhism. About two hundred books—both original and translations—are ascribed to him; among them were the following eighty-three Tantric books in Sanskrit:

'Sri-cakra-saṁbara-sādhana.'[1]

'Sri-bhagavadabhisamaya-nāma.'[2]

[1] *Catalogue du Fond tibétain*, II, p. 45.
[2] *Ibid.*, II, p. 46.

'Êka-vîra-sādhana-nāma.'[1]
'Vajrāsana-vajra-gîti.'[1]
'Vajrāsana-vajra-gîti-vrtti.'[1]
'Carya-gîta.'[1]
'Carya-gîti-vrtti.'[2]
'Vajra-yoginî-stotra.'[3]
'Ratnālaṁkara-siddhi.'[3]
'Vajra-yoginî-stotra.'[4]
'Sri-vajra-yoginî-sādhana-nāma.'[5]
'Vajra-vārāhī-sādhana.'[5]
'Bali-vidhi.'[6]
'Sri-hêvajra-sādhana-ratnāloka-nāma.'[7]
'Tri-ratna-tārā-stotra.'[8]
'Sri-mahā-kāla-bali-nāma.'[9]
'Bodhi-citta-mahā-sukhāmṅāya.[10]
'Sri-guhya-samāja-lokêsvara-sādhana-nāma.'[11]
'Aryāvalokitā-lokêsvara-sādhana.'[11]

[1] *Catalogue du Fond tibétain*, II, p. 46.
[2] *Ibid.*, II, p. 47.
[3] „ p. 64, Translated by the author.
[4] „ p. 65.
[5] „ p. 65.
[6] „ p. 87.
[7] „ p. 89.
[8] „ p. 115.
[9] „ p. 128.
[10] „ p. 125. Translated by the author.
[11] „ p. 154. „ „

'Sri-guhya-samāja-sṭotṭrā.'[1]
'Vairocana-yamāpyurpāyīkā nāma.'[2]
'Kṛsṇa-yamāri-sādhana-nāma.'[3]
'Vaja-dāka-yoginî-sādhana-nāma.'[3]
'Ratna-sambhava-yamāri-sādhana nāma.'[4]
'Amitābha-hṛdaya-rāga-yamāri-sādhana nāma.'[4]
'Vajra-tîkṣṇa-yamāri-sādhana nāma.'[4]
'Vajra-carcikā-sādhana nāma.'[5]
'Vajra-gîti-sukhardhā sādhana nāma.'[5]
'Karma-vajra-gîri-sādhana nāma.'[5]
'Mudgara-krodha-yamāri-sādhana nāma.'[6]
'Daṇḍa-dhṛgvidāra-yamāri-nāma-sādhana.'[6]
'Cnḍa-khaḍga-yamāri-sādhana-nāma.'[6]
'Prajñā-sukha-padma-yamāri-sādhana nāma.'[6]
'Saṁsāra-mano-niryāṇîkāra-nāma-saṁgîti.'[7]
'Dharma-dhātu-darsaṇa-gîti.'[7]
'Kāya-vāka-citta-supratisthā-nāma.'[8]

[1] *Catalogue du Fond tibétain*, II, p. 155. Translated by the author.
[2] *Ibid.*, II, p. 163.
[3] „ p. 164.
[4] „ p. 163.
[5] „ p. 164.
[6] „ p. 165.
[7] „ p. 227.
[8] „ p. 257.

'Bhagavad-kṣobhya-sādhana.'[1]
'Aksobhy-sādhana nāma.'[1]
'Sarva-karmāvaraṇa-visodhana-nāma-maṇḍala-vidhi.'[1]
'Homa-vidhi.'[2]
'Siddhê-kavira-mañju-ghoṣa-sādhana.'[3]
'Sri-vajra-pāṇi-sṭoṭra.'[4]
'Mṛta-sattva-pāpa-nirmocakasava-samskāra-vidhi viṣa-sputhi-prakāsa-darpaṇa-nāma.'[5]
'Nāga-sādhana-ratna-hiranya-siddhi-nāma.'[6]
'Nāga-prāṇāgni-sri-cakra-nāma nāga-vidā-rakahrcchula-vyuha.'[6]
'Ārya-haya-grîva-sādhana nāma.'[7]
'Sri-haya-grîra-sādhana.'[7]
'Āryā-cala-krodha-rāja-sṭoṭra.'[7]
'Sarva-tathāgaṭa-samaya-rakṣā-sādhana.'[8]
'Vimaloṣṇêṣa-dhāranî-vidhi.'[8]
'Bhaisajya-gurupāyikā sarva-karmāvaraṇa-visodhana.'[9]

[1] *Catalogue du Fond tibétain*, II, p. 289.
[2] *Ibid.*, II, p. 290.
[3] „ p. 299. Translated by the author.
[4] „ p. 327.
[5] „ p. 349.
[6] „ p. 353.
[7] „ p. 356.
[8] „ p. 359.
[9] „ p. 369.

'Aṣta-bhaya-trāṅa.'[1]
'Ārya-tārā-sṭoṭra.'[1]
'Ārya-tārā-sādhana.'[1]
'Sarva-saṁaya-samgraha nāma.'[2]
'Ārya-gaṅapati-rāga-vajra-samaya-stotra nāma.'[3]
'Jala-bali-vimala-grantha.'[4]
'Nāga-bali-vidhi.'[4]
'Ārya-saṇḍakṣarî-sādhana.'[5]
'Khasaparṅāvalokitā-sādhana.'[6]
'Mahā-yaksa-sênāpati-nîlāmbaradhara-vajra-pāṅi-sādhana-nāma.'[7]
'Mantrārthāvatāra.'[8]
'Samaya-gupti.'[9]
'Sandha-dāna.'[9]
'Homa-vidhi.'[9]
'Dêva-pūjā-krama.'[9]
'Mṛtyu-vaṅcana.'[9]

[1] *Catalogue du Fond tibétain*, III, p. 76.
[2] *Ibid.*, III, p. 85.
[3] ,, p. 88.
[4] ,, p. 97.
[5] ,, p. 178.
[6] ,, p. 179.
[7] ,, p. 180.
[8] ,, p. 183.
[9] ,, p. 184.

'Āyuḥ-sādhana.'[1]
'Mumūrṣū-sāstra.'[1]
'Sapta-parva-vidhi.'[2]
'Città-vidhi.'[2]
'Satya-dvayāvatāra.'[3]
'Êka-smrtyupadêsa.'[4]
'Madhyamakopadêsa nāma.'[4]
'Ratna-karaṇḍodghāta nāma madhyamakopadêsa.'[4]
'Madhyamakopadêsa nāma.'[5]
'Bodhisattva-carya-sutrî-kṛtāvavāda.'[6]
'Bodhipatha-pradîpa.'[6]
'Bodhi-mārga-pradîpa-pañjikā nāma.'[6]
'Garbha-samgraha nāma.'[7]
'Hṛdaya-niksepa nāma.'[7]
'Bodhi-sattva-mañyāvali.'[7]
'Bodhi-sattva-caryā-sutra-kṛtāvavāda.'[7]

He translated the following twenty-two books into Tibetan :

'Satvarādhanā stava.'[8]

[1] *Catalogue du Fond tibétain*, III, p. 184.
[2] *Ibid.*, III, p. 308.
[3] " p. 314.
[4] " p. 321.
[5] " p. 322.
[6] " p. 327.
[7] " p. 328.
[8] *Ibid.*, II, p. 5.

'Abhi samaya-vibhanga nāma.'[1]
'Sri-cakra-samkara-sādhana.'[2]
'Sri-bhagavadabhi-samaya-nāma.'[3]
'Vajrāsana vajra-gîti vṛtti.'[3]
'Kulikamāta tattva-nirnaya nāma.'[4]
'Vajra-yoginî-stotra.'[5]
'Tri-ratna-tārā-stotra.'[6]
'Sri-guhya-samāja-lokesvara-sādhana nāma.'[7]
'Krṣṇa-yamāri-sādhana.'[8]
'Mṛtyu-vañcanopadesa.'[9]
'Sri-guhya-samāja-stotra.'[1]
'Kāya-vāka-cittasupratisthā-nāma.'[2]
'Aryāsta-bhaya-trāta-nāma-tārā-sādhana.'[3]
'Tārā-bhattārikā-sādhana.'[4]
'Sarva-samaya-samgsaha-nāma.'[5]

[1] *Catalogue du Fond tibétain*, II, p. 6.
[2] *Ibid.*, II, p. 45.
[3] „ p. 46.
[4] „ p. 57.
[5] „ p. 64.
[6] „ p. 115.
[7] „ p. 154.
[8] „ p. 162.
[9] „ p. 126.
[1] „ p. 155.
[2] „ p. 257.
[3] *Ibid.*, III, p. 72.
[4] „ p. 75.
[5] „ p. 85.

'Caturmahārāja-bali-nāma.'[1]
'Amṛtoḍaya nāma balividhi.'[2]
'Jala-bali-vimala-grantha.'[3]
'Nāga-bali-vidhi.'[3]
'Kṛṣṇa-yamāri-cakrodyaota.'[4]
'Cakra-nāma.'[5]

(10.)

VIRYASIṀHA

Pandita Viryasiṁha was the contemporary of the great Buddhist reformer, Atisa or Dipaṁkara. He helped this great sage in the translating of his 'Saṁsāra-manonirnayāṇī-kāra-nāma-saṁgīti'. This Tibetan translation was made at the Vihāra of Vikramasīlā.[6]

Viryasiṁha was associated with Ācārya Dipaṁkara Sri Jñāna in the translation into

[1] *Catalogue du Fond tibétain*, III, p. 95.
[2] *Ibid.*, III, p. 96. ⎧ He was also the author of these books
[3] " p. 97. ⎩ " " "
[4] " p. 164.
[5] " p. 165.
[6] " p. 338.

Tibetan of 'Kāya-vākacițța-supratistā-nāma also'[1] in his capacity of interpreter of the Tibetan language. This work was also carried out at Vikramasīlā.

It thus appears that he was connected with the University of Vikramasīlā. We do not know anything more about him. As a colleague of the great monk Atisa, he must have flourished in the eleventh century A.D.; because Atisa's dates are—birth A.D. 980 and death A.D. 1053.

He was perhaps the translator of the Tibetan version of 'Jātaka-mālā-pañjikā,'[2] but M. P. Cordier holds that most probably the name Viryasiṁha, the translator, is a misprint for Vidyāsiṁha or Vidyākara Siṁha.

One book, the 'Dêvîtārêkaviṁsati-sțoțra Visuddha-cuḍāmaṇi-nāma,'[3] was rendered

[1] *Catalogue du Fond tibétain*, II, p. 257.

[2] *Ibid.*, III, p. 512.

[3] *Ibid.*, II, p. 114.

into Tibetan solely by him, its author was Mahācārya Suryagupta.

Though he was not as great a worker in the cause of Buddhism as Atisa, yet he popularised Buddhist Literature in Tibet by his translations. His influence, in its own small way, was effective.

(11.)

ABHAYAKARA GUPTA

Abhayakara Gupta was a great pandit of Vikramasīlā University. He bore the title of Siḍḍha Mahā Pandita. His influence on Tibetan thought was also very great; and he is even now worshipped as a great saint by the Buddhists. His biography has been included by Rai S. C. Das Bahadur in the 'Lives of the Panchhen-Rinpochhes' or 'Tāsi Lamas'.[1]

Following the Tibetan tradition Rai S. C. Das Bahadur holds that Abhayaka Gupta was

[1] J. A. S. B., 1882, pp. 16—18.

born about the middle of the ninth century of the Christian Era near the city of Gaṇḍa in Bengal. But we find that one of his works, 'Muni-maṭālaṁkāra,' was composed in the thirtieth year of the reign of Crimad Rāma Pāla, the King of Bengal. The book is dated, according to M. P. Cordier, A.D. 1125.[1] King Rāma Pāla, according to Tibetan authorities, flourished during A.D. 1092—1138.[2] If he came to the throne in the year 1092 Abhaya-kara composed the book in the year A.D. 1122; but V. Smith places Rāmapāla's date as A.D. 1084—1130. If so, the book must have been written in the year A.D. 1114. It can be assumed from this, that Abhayakara flourished towards the end of the eleventh century and at the beginning of the twelfth century.

Abhayakara Gupta, who came from Gaṇḍa, was educated in the country of Magadha,

[1] Cordier—*Catalogue*, III, p. 314.
[2] Vidyabhusan's *Indian Logic*, p. 149.

which was at that time under the sway of King Rāma Pāla. After learning the five sciences, he joined the order of monks and soon became famous as a great pandit. King Rāma Pāla invited him to perform the religious ceremonies in his palace. As a monk, he worked hard; he wrote sāstras in the first two watches of the day, and explained the principles of Dharma in the third.

There is a story told in Tibetan books about a Dākini who, disguised as a girl, tried to tempt Abhayakara Gupta. He was, however, more than a match for her wiles. His stern morality pleased the Dākini so much that she blessed him thus: "You will obtain fore-knowledge during the interval between your death and re-birth. As a step towards its acquirement you must write many works on the 'Dharma Sāstras'." She also drew his attention to the practice of making tantric maṇḍalas or ritualistic circles. Tibetans who believe in this story think that this incident inspired Abhayakara Gupta to compose several sastric works and commentaries.

Another story is told of him, how he visited the city of Chara Simha, where the Chandāla King was about to make a hundred human sacrifices to his horrid god. The appearance of a hideous snake over his head, created by magic, terrified the Chandāla King so much that he set his victims free at the request of Abhayakara Gupta. These stories are introduced by Tibetans only to add glory to his saintly character.

Buddhism was in a flourishing condition about this time. There were three thousand monks at the Vikramasīlā monastery, one thousand at Vajrāsana (Buddha Gaya), and a thousand more at the Odantapuri University. On the occasion of religious Festivals, more than five thousand monks would assemble, including both mahāyānists and srāvakas. The number of srāvakas all over the country, was, however, so large that it exceeded ten thousand.

King Rāma Pāla, who was ruling Bengal and Magadha at this time, was a great patron of Buddhism. He allowed free food every day to forty mahāyānists and two hundred srāvakas, belonging to Vajrāsana (Buddha Gaya).

Though Abhayakara Gupta was the head of the monks belonging to the mahāyāna school, he was respected also by the srāvakas. He remained at the Vikramasīlā monastery for a long time. In his day the University of Vikramasīlā was under the protection of the son of King Subhasri of Eastern India (perhaps the Eastern districts of Magadha). It is said, on the authority of Tibetan writers, that a *Turushka* war took place at this time. According to Sarat Ch. Das, this war perhaps refers to the invasion of the earlier Mahomedans under the Kalifs. It is also stated that Abhayakara Gupta played an important part in this war against the *Turushkas.* He invoked several of the Dharma Pālas (*i.e.*, the spiritual protectors of the world) and transformed the offerings with their help into eagles, who turned out the *Turushkas*.[1]

Like Dipaṁkara, Abhayakara Gupta was a great writer, as well as translator, of Buddhist scriptures. He was proficient in Tibetan, translating into Tibetan several of his own books in Sanskrit. Some of his writings appear in the catalogue of Tibetan Tripitaka under the name of Abhayakara Gupta and others under that of Abhayakara. He seems also to have been associated with the famous University of Nālandā, where he translated a few books.

[1] Sarat Ch. Das—" Contributions on the Religion and History of Tibet." J.A.S.B., 1882, p. 18.

The question whether Abhayakara personally visited Tibet, remains still to be decided. It seems, however, probable that he did, because he is worshipped even now as a saint there. He translated these seven books into Tibetan:

'Sri-mahā-kāla-sādhana-nāma.'[1]
'Sri-mahā-kālāntara-sādhana-nāma.'[1]
'Siddhaēka-vīra-sādhana.'[2]
'Vajra-yāga-mulāpatti-karma-sastra.'[3]
'Kāli-sūrya-cakra-vasa [kriyā] nāma.'[4]
'Gaṇa-cakra-pūjā-krama-nāma.'[5]
'Saṁksipta-vajra-vārāho-sādhana.'[6]

It is interesting to note that all these books belonged to the *Rgyud-hgrel* or Tantra group. He was a great Tantric scholar. The book 'Abhisêka-Prakarana'[7] was composed in Sanskrit and translated into Tibetan by him.

[1] *Catalogue du Fond tibétain*, II, p. 127.
[2] *Ibid.*, II, p. 379.
[3] *Ibid.*, III, p. 85.
[4] ,, p. 219.
[5] ,, p. 246.
[6] ,, p. 257.
[7] ,, p. 47.

He is reputed to be the author of twenty-six more books, which were translated into Tibetan by various hands :

'Sri-kāla-cakroddāna.'[1]
'Sri-cakra-sambarābhi samaya.'[2]
'Swādhisthāna-kramopadêsa-nāma.'[2]
'Cakra-ṣambarābhi-samayopadesa.'[2]
'Sri-sampuṭa-tantra-rāja-tīkā āmnāya-mañjarī nāma.'[3]
'Sri-Buddha-kapāla-mahā-tantra-rāja-tikā Abhaya-Paddhati-nāma.'[4]
'Pañca-krama-mata-tīkā-candra-prabhā-nāma.'[5]
'Rakta-yamāntaka-nispanna-yoga-nāma.'[6]
'Gaṇa-cakra-vidhi-nāma.'[7]
'Vajra-yānāpatti-mañjarī-nāma.'[8]
'Vajrāvali-nāma-maṇdalopāyikā.'[9]
'Nispanna-yogāvali-nāma.'[10]

1 *Catalogue du Fond tibétain*, II, p. 22.
2 *Ibid.*, III, p. 47.
3 *Ibid.*, II, p. 71.
4 „ p. 107.
5 „ p. 142.
6 „ p. 180.
7 „ p. 256.
8 „ p. 255.
9 „ p. 370.
10 „ p. 371.

'Jyoti-manjari-nāma-homāyika.'[1]
'Ucusma jambhala-sādhana-nāma.'[2]
'Bodhi-paddhati-nāma.'[3]
'Sri-mahākāla-karma-sambhāra.'[4]
'Vajra-mahākāla-karmoccālā-nābhicāra-nāma.'[4]
'Vajra-mahākāla-karma-vibhangābhicāra-nāma.'[4]
'Vajra-mahākāla-karma-kāya-stam bhanābhicāra-nāma.'[4]
'Vajra-mahākāla-karma-vāka-stambhanābhicāra-nama.'[4]
'Vajra-mahākāla-karma-ciṭṭā-stambhanābhicāra-nāma.'[5]
'Vajra mahākāla-karma-vaṣosṇābhisāya-nāma.'[5]
'Vajra-mahākalā-karmābhicāra pratisamjīvana ṣānti-karman-nāma.'[5]
'Upadesa-mañjari-nāma-sarva-tantratpannappunasāmānyabhāsya.'[5]

[1] *Catalogue du Fond tibétain*, II, p. 371.
[2] *Ibid.*, III, p. 89.
[3] „ p. 94.
[4] „ p. 209.
[5] „ p. 210.

These books also belonged to the Tantra group. It should be remembered that Vikramasīlā was a great centre of the Tantra cult, and Abhayakara Gupta appears to have been one of its keenest followers. Besides these, two works of the *Mdo-Hgrel* or sutra group were written by him :

'Aryāsṭa-sāhasrikā-prajñā-pāramitā-vṛtti marmakoumudī nāma.'[1]

'Muni-matālaṁkāra.'[2]

Yet another book, 'Vajra-mahā-kālabhicāra-homa-nāma'[3] might be attributed to the great pandit Nāgārjuna; but it is more probable that our monk Abhayakara Gupta collected together the instructions of Nāgārjuna and compiled this book.

Abhayakara bore the well-known title of Ārya-Mahā Paṇḍita. His name in Tibetan is Hgigs-med-hbyun-gnas sbas-pahi-shabs, and

[1] *Catalogue du Fond tibétain*, III, p. 282.
[2] *Ibid.*, III, p. 314.
[3] „ p. 210.

his influence on Tibetan Buddhism was very great. He inspired many followers with the noble ideal of the Lord Buddha, and for all his services he is still remembered and worshipped by them.

(12.)

TATHĀGATA RAKSITA

This great pandit also gave his quota to the development of Buddhism in Tibet and India. As he belonged to the University of Vikramasīlā, he bore both the titles of Mahāpandita and Upādhyāya. Through his books on Tantra, he tried to popularise the Tantra cult.

Tathāgata Raksita was a native of Bhachama (?) which is placed by M. P. Cordier in the country of Orissa (Oḍiviṣa). He came from a *Kāyasthavamsa*, though the members of his family were medical men by profession.[1]

[1] Cordier—*Catalogue*, II, p. 32.

The Lama Tārānātha makes only a passing reference to this monk from Orissa in his 'History of Buddhism in India'.[1] He speaks of Tathāgata Raksita as the Tantra-ācārya of Vikramasīlā along with Jñānapāda, Dipaṁkara-bhadra, Sridhara, Bhavabhadra and others; and includes his name among the list of eminent professors of Vikramasīlā. Tathāgata Raksita came to the Vihāra after Kṛsna-samajaradschra.

As he was a Tantra-ācārya, naturally, most of his works relate to the Buddhist Tantras. The books he translated into Tibetan of his own and also of other monks prove his great scholarship.

Tathāgata Rakṣita (called in Tibetan De-bshin gçegs-pahi sruṅ-ba) was the author as well as the translator (into Tibetan) of seven books:

'Sragdharā-sādhana.'[2]

[1] Schiefner's *Tārānātha* (1869), p. 259.
[2] *Catalogue du Fond tibétain*, II, p. 161.

'Sunyatā-bhāvanā.'[1]
'Kudṛsti-dusaṇa.'[1]
'Caura-bandha.'[1]
'Vidyā-vardhana.'
'Mṛtyu-kāpaṭya.'[1]
'Yoginî-saṁcārya-nirbandha.'[2]

He composed also two books on Tantra in Sanskrit (rendered into Tibetan by other monks):

'Sri-vajra-bhairava-hasṭa-cimhaṇa-visudhi-nāma.'[3]
'Catura-mukha-samaya-siddhi-sādhana-nāma.'[4]

The following books, in their original Sanskrit, did not come from the pen of Tathāgata Rakṣita, but were rendered by him into Tibetan:

'Sri-hêrukābhyuḍaya-mahā-yogīnī-gīta-Tantra-rāja-katipayākṣara-panjikā.'[5]

[1] *Catalogue du Fond tibétain*, II, p. 161.
[2] *Ibid.*, II, p. 32.
[3] ,, p. 174.
[4] ,, p. 196.
[5] *Ibid.*, II, p. 32. [The Tibetan version of this book was executed by our monk at the University of Dpal (Sri) Vikramasilā].

'Abhisêka-prakaraṇa.'[1]
'Sri-vajra-bhaîrava-tantra-tippaṅî-nama.'[2]
'Vajra-bhaîrava-tantra-paṅjikā.'[3]

The date of Tathāgata Rakṣita remains still to be decided by further research.

(13.)

RATNAKIRTI

Ratnakirti was another pandit associated with the monastery of Vikramasīlā. In the catalogue of Tibetan Tripitaka he appears as Ratnakirti of Vikramasīlā, the author of 'Kalyāṇa-kāṇḍa-prakaraṇa-nāma.'[4] He was at Vikramasīlā with Jetari and other pandits and it was from him while there that Ratnākara Sānti learned the Sutra and Tantra. If we fix the date of Ratnākara Sānti at A.D. 915—983 then we can say that his *guru*

[1] *Catalogue du Fond tibétain*, II, p. 155.
[2] *Ibid.*, II, p. 168.
[3] „ p. 169.
[4] *Ibid.*, III, p. 391.

Ratnakirti was flourishing in the early part of the tenth century A.D.

He also was a great Tibetan scholar and translated some of his own books as well as those of others into Tibetan. Through these translations, he was able to enrich Tibetan literature and to propagate the spirit of Indian Buddhism in Tibet.

He was the author as well as the translator of three books:

'Dharma-viniscaya-prakaraṇa-nāma.'[1]
'Abhisamayālaṁkāra-vṛtti kîrti-kalā-nāma.'[2]
'Kuru-kullā-karma-yogopadêsa.'[3]

It may be that there was another Ratnakirti, a native of Khamspa (the eastern part of Tibet), who was responsible for the translation of more than ninety Sanskrit books on Buddhism into Tibetan.

[1] *Catalogue du Fond tibétain*, III, p. 392.
[2] *Ibid.*, III, p. 280.
[3] ,, p. 129. The text was transmitted to Ratnakirti by Amoghavajra.

The Ratnakirti who belonged to Vikramasīlā bore the titles of Pandita and Mahā Pandita. He is also described as the Upādhyāya of India. His name in Tibetan was Rin-chen-grags.

(14.)

MANJUSRI

Manjusri is also best known by his translations. The scene of his work on these translations from the Sanskrit was happily the great Vihāra of Vikramasīlā. He was perhaps an ardent devotee of the goddess Tārā, because he translated two books relating to her. One was, 'Tārā-dêvî-stotra Akaviṁsaka-Sādhananāma.[1] The other was, 'Arya-tārā-bhattārika-sādhana Sakalpâika-viṁsaka-karma-saṁkṣêpa nāma.'[1] Both these were the original works of Acārya Surya Gupta of Kasmira. Though the originals are now lost, the translations in Tibetan remain. Another

[1] *Catalogue du Fond tibétain*, II, p. 113.

book translated by him was, 'Vajrācarya-kṛiyā-samuccaya' written by Pandit Avadhuta Srimaj Jagaddarpaṇa.[1]

He also bore the well-known title of Paṇḍita.

(15.)

DHARMA KIRTI

One of the effects of the introduction of Buddhism into Tibet was the arrival in India of some Tibetan monks for the study of Buddhist scriptures. They came to the monasteries of Vikramasīlā, Nālanda and Jagaddala to learn Sanskrit and to study the Buddhistic literature in that language—one such monk from Tibet was Dharma Kirti.

Dharma Kirti was a popular name among the Buddhists. One Dharma Kirti is known as one of the greatest Buddhist logicians. It is doubtful whether that Dharma Kirti, however, was associated with the Vikramasīlā

[1] *Catalogue du Fond tibétain*, III, p. 226.

University, rather he may have had some relation with Nālanda, because, it is said, he studied under Ācārya Dharmapāla, who preceded Ācārya Silabhadra in the directorate of that University.[1] He could not have had any connection with Vikramasīlā Vihāra, as he (a disciple of Dignāga) flourished in the seventh century A.D., and that University was established a century later (eighth century) by King Dharma Pāla.

We have, therefore, to look for the other Dharma Kirti. He was rather closely associated with the Vikramasīlā monastery, because we find it stated that he translated the Sanskrit book 'Samaya Pañca' of Ācārya Padma Sambhava Pāda at that Vihāra.[2]

Although the name of this monk is Indian, he seems to have been a Tibetan; because we find that he was a native of Khams (or Khams-pa)

[1] S. C. Vidyabhusan's *Indian Logic*, p. 103.

[2] *Catalogue du Fond tibétain*, II, pp. 75—6.

which, as Sarat Ch. Das says, is the eastern part of Tibet. He is also described as a Lotsaba, that is, a Tibetan scholar versed in the Sanskrit language. It appears, therefore, that he was a Tibetan monk, who came to Vikramasīlā to study Sanskrit. He subsequently translated various Sanskrit books into Tibetan:

'Kāla-cakrāvatāra nāma.'[1]

'Ārya-mañju-sri-nāma-saṁgîti-vṛtti amṛta-bindu-pratyā-lokā nāma.'[2]

'Samaya-pañca.'[3]

'Sri-Buddha-kapāla-mahā-tantra-rāja-tîkā Abhaya-paddhati nāma.'[4]

'Astādasa-patala-vyākhyāna.'[5]

'Daṣa-tattva.'[6]

'Vādi-rāja-sādhana.'[7]

[1] *Catalogue du Fond tibétain*, II, p. 22. (He was helped by the author, Abhayakara Gupta.)

[2] *Ibid.*, II, p. 25. (In this case he only acted as an interpreter to the real translator, Sugatasri of Kasmira.)

[3] „ pp. 75—76.

[4] „ p. 107.

[5] „ p. 145.

[6] „ p. 155.

[7] *Ibid.*, III, pp. 4—5.

'Mahā-rāja-ḍīḍa-mañjusri-sādhana.'[1]
'Vidyādhara-pitaka-saṁkṣipta-mañjusrî-sādhana.'[1]
'Mañjusrî-prajñapakrama.'[1]
'Vajrānaṅga-mañju-ghosa-sādhana.'[2]
'Dharma-dhātu-vāgîsvara-sādhana.'[2]
'Ārya-mañju-vajra-siddhaîka-vîra-sādhana.'
'Mañju-sri-prajñācakra-sādhana.'[2]
'Sadyo-anubhvārapachana-sādhana.'[3]
'Kṛsna-yamāri-sādhana.'[3]

Dharma Kirti was the contemporary of Abhayakara Gupta. He helped him in translating 'Kāla-cakrāvatāra-nāma'; so he flourished towards the end of the eleventh century and the beginning of the twelfth century A.D.

(16.)

SĀKYA SRI BHADRA

Mahāpandita Sākya Sri Bhadra was the last monk of the Vikramasīlā University to visit

[1] *Catalogue du Fond tibétain*, III, p.5.
[2] *Ibid.*, III, p. 6.
[3] „ p. 7.

Tibet. The fatal Moslem conquest of Magadha drove him there for shelter. He belonged to the Kingdom of Kashmira. In his own time he became famous as a great logician. Pandits like Buddha-sri of Nepal, Ācārya Ratnarakṣita, Jñānakara Gupta, Buddha-sri-mitra and others were his contemporaries. He was flourishing, according to the Tibetan authorities, in the time of the King Rāthikasena. It is difficult to say who this Rāthikasena was. Presumably he was a scion of the Sena family. We do not know when he reigned, perhaps just on the eve of the Moslem conquest. He was succeeded by Lavasena. Is he the same as Lakṣmana Sena?

At this time, says Lama Tārānātha, appeared a Turuska King, Chandra (?), in the territory between the rivers Ganges and Jamna. He joined forces with another in Bengal and conquered the whole land of Magadha, and killed many priests (bhikshus) of the Viharas of Odantapuri and Vikramasīlā.

This certainly refers to the invasion of Bakhtiar Khilji about 1203, because we know that he was the Turuska who destroyed the University of Vikramasīlā. Then we may suggest that King Lavasena is perhaps Lakṣmana Sena in whose time the fatal invasion of Bakhtiar Khiliji took place. Our monk perhaps witnessed the sack of this great centre of Indian culture by the Moslems. The account of the destruction of the great Vihāra has been preserved by the author of 'Tabakāt-i-Nāṣiri'. We read: "The greater number of the inhabitants of that place were Brahmanas (bhikshus ?), and the whole of those Brahmanas had their heads shaven; and they were all slain. There were a great number of books on the religion of the Hindus (Buddhists ?) there; and when all these books came under the observation of the Musalmans, they summoned a number of Hindus that they might give them information respecting the import of those books; but the whole of the Hindus had been killed. On becoming acquainted [with the contents of those books], it was found that the whole of that fortress and city was a college, and in the Hindu tongue, they call a college, Bihār (a Buddhist monastery)."[1]

After the destruction of the Vikramasīlā monastery, Pandit Sākya Sri Bhadra went to the University of Jagaddala, whence he visited Tibet.[2] Many other monks, it is said, followed him and went over to Tibet, where they passed the remainder of their lives preaching the sacred doctrines of Lord Buddha.

He was a Tibetan scholar as well, and translated two books into that language:

'Tārā-sādhanopadêsa-krama.'[3]

'Bhagavatî-tārā-dêvyêkaviṁsati-stotrapāyikā.'[4]

[1] Major H. G. Raverty's Trans. of *Tabakāt-i-Nāṣari* (1881), Vol. I, p. 552.

[2] A. Schiefner's *Tārānātha*, p. 255.

[3] *Catalogue du Fond tibétain*, II, pp. 113—4.

[4] *Ibid.*, III, p. 114.

He was the author of the following books:

'Sri-kāla-cakra-gaṇanopadesa-nāma.'[1]
'Paṅca-graha-prati-gaṅanopadesa-nāma.'[1]
'Ārya-tārā-sādhana.'[2]
'Visudha-darsaṅa-cayopadesa-nāma.'[3]
'Nāma-samgîtī-vacanopadesa-nāma.'[4]
'Maṅjusrî-cala-cakra.'[5]
'Samkṣiptāmoghapāsa-sādhana.'[6]

Two works appear under the name of Sākya Sri, who might be the same as Sākya Sri Bhadra:

'Siṁha-nāda-rakṣā-cakra-nāma.'[7]
'Kāla-pūjā-mahā-catuksa-kārikā.'[8]

---

1 *Catalogue du Fond tibétain*, II, p. 23.
2 *Ibid.*, II, pp. 120—1.
3 ,, p. 251.
4 ,, p. 281.
5 ,, p. 300.
6 ,, pp. 321—2.
7 ,, p. 321.
8 ,, p. 13.

CHAPTER IV

PANDITS OF NĀLANDA

THE site of the University of Nālanda was the modern village of Baragaon, seven miles north of Rajgir, in Behar.[1] The monastery which grew up in the village of Nālanda became one of the greatest centres of Buddhist culture. Before the village came into prominence as a great vihāra, many learned pandits like Nāgārjuna and Arya Deva helped in the development of the future University. When Fahien, the Chinese traveller visited the village of Nalo, in the fourth century A.D., the University was not yet completed. In the

[1] Cunningham's *Ancient Geography of India*, p. 498.

seventh century, it had already become a centre of Indian culture to which famous Chinese travellers like Yuan Chwang and It-sing came to learn Sanskrit, and to study the Buddhist scriptures from Indian ācāryas like Dharmapāla and Silabhadra. In the seventh century, the Chinese monk Ou-Ko'ng and, later on, Ki-ye also visited the great monastery of Nālanda.

This University sent missionaries to China and to Tibet. It was also a great centre of Tibetan learning. Indian pandits learned Tibetan in this monastery and translated numerous Buddhist books from the Sanskrit. Through these translations they instilled the principles of Buddhism in Tibet.

Prominent pandits like Ācārya Padmasambhava and Sānta Rakshita went to Tibet to spread the teachings of Lord Buddha at the invitation of the Tibetan King Khri-sroṅ-deutsan (A.D. 728—786).

We shall deal here with the following pandits who were associated with the Nālanda University:

Mahācārya Arya Deva; Dharmapāla; Ācārya Silabhadra; Chandra Gomin; Padma Sambhava; Sānta Raksita; Buddhakirti; Karna Sri; Sumati Sena; Karnapati; Mahāyogin Kumāra Sri; Sthiramati.

(1.)

ARYA DEVA

Arya Deva, who bore the title of Mahācārya, was one of the earliest pandits of Nālanda. He was responsible for the foundation of this University. His influence on Tibet and her culture was great, and his books are popular among the Tibetan Buddhists.

The account of his life has been preserved by Lama Tārānātha in his 'History of Indian Buddhism'.[1] Arya Deva was sometimes known

[1] A. Schiefner's *Tārānātha*, pp. 83—6 and 93.

simply as Deva. The Chinese traveller Yuan Chwang speaks of him in his Travels[1] and narrates how Arya Deva became the disciple of Nāgārjuna. Arya Deva had come to have a discussion with the sage. Nāgārjuna sent to Deva a bowl full of water. Deva dropped a needle into the bowl. Seeing that, Nāgārjuna exclaimed: "He is a wise man!" When his disciple asked him why he said so, Nāgārjuna replied that the bowl full of water typified his own universal knowledge, and the dropping of the needle signified Deva's comprehension of all knowledge. He then invited him to a discussion about the mysteries of Buddhism. Deva tried to discuss, but failed. He thereupon submitted himself as a disciple, and Nāgārjuna afterwards initiated him into the mysteries of Buddhism.

After finishing his education under the Sage, Deva obtained permission from his *guru*

[1] Walters—*Yuan Chwang*, II, pp. 200—1.

to proceed to Magadha to engage in discussion with a Tirthaka, and was successful.

We know, on the authority of Lama Tārānātha, that Arya Deva was a great pandit of the University of Nālanda. It may therefore, be asked: "Was the University of Nālanda established at the time when Arya Deva flourished?" We have first to settle the date of Arya Deva. If, according to Tārānātha, he was the contemporary of Chandra Gupta, then he flourished in the fourth century A.D. When Fa-hien visited India, he found the University only in process of development in the village of Nalo, so that in Arya Deva's time the full glory and splendour of the University had not yet come. It was then in the course of evolution. Arya Deva may have been one of the pandits who laboured hard in the early days of Nālanda to make of it the renowned University that it eventually became, accommodating ten thousand students.

He composed three books, which reached Tibet in their Tibetan version:

'Sātaka-sāstra.'
'Bhrama-pramathana-yukti-hetu-siddhi.'
'Madhyamaka-bhrama-ghāta-nāma.'[1]

The last book was composed at the great Vihāra of Nālanda at the request of Hdsam-buhi-gliṅ-gi-rgyal-po, (Jambudvipa Rāja), Sukhacarya (*alias* Udayi, Sadvaha). It was translated into Tibetan by Upādhya Dipaṁkara Sri Jṅāṅa (born in A.D. 980).

(2.)

SĪLABHADRA

The famous Chinese traveller, Yuan Chwang, has preserved for us the account of the life of Acārya Sīlabhadra, who presided over the University of Nālanda. He was the *guru* of Yuan Chwang, who learned Sanskrit from him in the monastery of Nālanda.[2] As

[1] *Catalogue du Fond tibétain*, III, p. 298.
[2] Walters—*Yuan Chwang*, Vol. II, p. 109.

he was in such close touch with him, he was able to note down the details of his *guru's* life. Another Chinese traveller, It-sing, also visited Nālanda, and speaks of him.

Ācārya Sīlabhadra, says Yuan Chwang, was the son of the king of Samaṭaṭa (Eastern Bengal). He came from a Brahmanical family. Young Sīlabhadra was very fond of learning. He sought it throughout India before he came to the famous Nālanda University. At that time Ācārya Dharmapāla was presiding over the monastery, and he found in him a zealous student of Buddhism. Dharmapāla Pusa took him as his disciple, instructed him in the Buddhist scriptures, and in course of time, he was ordained as a bhikshu. Soon Sīlabhadra's fame spread far and wide. When he was thirty years old, a learned but proud Brahmin came from Southern India to engage Dharmapāla in a religious discussion. When the Brahmin came, Sīlabhadra the most eminent of the disciples of Dharmapāla proposed to accept the challenge. He was allowed and was successful in defeating that Brahmana. When the king heard of his victory, he wanted to make the gift of a village to him. Sīlabhadra informed him : "The scholar with dyed garments is satisfied with the requisites of his Order; leading a life of purity and continence what has he to do with a city?" The king, however, pressed him to accept his gift "for the advancement of Buddhism," and he was persuaded to accept the gift for his church.

Yuan-chwang mentions Sīlabhadra, with Dharmapāla and Guṇamati, as the great Pusa who rendered valuable services to the cause of Buddhism.[1]

When did Sīlabhadra flourish? We know he was the *guru* of Yuan Chwang, who came to

[1] Walters, Vol. II, p. 168.

the Nālanda monastery in A.D. 635. It is certain that by A.D. 635 he had become Abbot of the Nālanda Vihāra and at that time he must have been at least fifty years old. We can, therefore, place his date at A.D. 585—640.

Ācārya Sīlabhadra was a great logician of the Buddhist School. Many of his works have not come down to us for we find only one in the whole Tibetan Tripitaka. That book was 'Arya-Buddha-bhumi-vyākhyāna'.[1] It was translated into Tibetan, but we do not know the name of the translator.

To the Tibetans Sīlabhadra was known as Slob-dpon (Acārya) Ṅaṅ-tshul-bzaṅ-po (Sīlabhadra).

(3.)

DHARMAPĀLA

Dharmapāla was Abbot of the University of Nālanda for a long time. He is mentioned

[1] *Catalogue du Fond tibétain*, III, p. 365.

by Yuan-Chwang as well as by It-sing. Yuan-Chwang says that he was one of the great *Pusas* (Bodhisattvas) of Nālanda, who rendered yeoman service to Buddhism by their expository commentaries.[1]

Dharmapāla was a native of Southern India, being born in Kanchipura. His father was the minister of that kingdom and when quite young he was asked by the king and queen to be present at a royal feast given in his honour. In the evening of that very day, however, he became oppressed with a sense of sorrow and, without attending the royal feast, took the monk's garb and left the world. He roamed about for a time and at last came to the monastery of Nālanda, where he was admitted as a monk. While there, he became proficient in the Buddhist scriptures and eventually rose to be the abbot of the Vihāra. Under him Ācarya Sīlabhadra studied. We have

[1] Watters, Vol. II, p. 168.

settled Acārya Sīlabhadra's date as A.D. 585—640. When Yuan-Chwang visited the Vihāra he had already vacated the post of abbot in favour of Sīlabhadra (A.D. 635). He must, therefore, have flourished between the middle of the sixth century and the early years of the seventh century. The Chinese traveller mentions the ruins of a monastery at Kausambi, the spot where Dharmapāla defeated the heretics in discussion.

Dharmapāla composed in Sanskrit a commentary on 'Candra Grammar' by Mahācārya Candragomin, which Vṛtti was known as 'Varṇa-sutra-vṛtti-nāma.'[1]

Dharmapāla was the author of four Buddhistic books in Sanskrit, which found their way into Tibet through their Tibetan versions:

'Ālambaṇa-pratyāya-dhyāna-sāstra-vyākhyā.'[2]

[1] *Catalogue du Fond tibétain*, III, p. 458.
[2] S. C. Vidyābhusan's *Indian Logic*, etc., p. 102.

'Vidyāmātra-siddhi-sāstra-vyākhyā.'[1]
'Sata-sāstra-vaipulya-vyākhyā.'[2]
'Vali-tattva-samgraha.'[3]

(4.)

CANDRAGOMIN

The great scholar Candragomin was associated in various ways with the University of Nālanda and numerous books which he produced on Buddhism, found their way into Tibet. They were very popular amongst the Buddhists, who translated them rapidly into Tibetan.

The account of his life appears in Lama Tarānātha's 'History of Indian Buddhism,'[3] and also in the Tibetan book 'Pag-sam-jon-zang'.[4] To the Tibetans he was known as Ācārya Zla-wa-ḍge-bṣṅen.

[1] S. C. Vidyābhusan's *Indian Logic*, etc., p. 141.

[2] *Catalogue du Fond tibétain*, II, p. 86.

[3] A. Schiefner's *Tārānātha*, pp. 145—146 and 148—158.

[4] S. C. Das' Edition, pp. 95—96, also Vidyabhusan's *Indian Logic*, pp. 121—123.

Born in a Ksattriya family of Varendra (North Bengal), Candragomin learned the Buddhist scriptures of the Sutra and Abhidharma from the ācārya Sthiramati. Later on he accepted the Buddhist faith from Ācārya Asoka, the author of a book on logic named 'Sāmānya-dūsana-dikprakāsikā'. The story is told of him that when he refused to marry the daughter of the King of Nālendra he was put into a chest and thrown into the river Ganges, and carried to an island near the ocean, where he was miraculously saved by the goddess Tāra.

He was a great traveller; through Ceylon and South India, he came to the Nālanda Vihāra. The monks were at first unwilling to take him in as he was a mere *upāsaka*; but Candrakirti persuaded them and arranged a grand reception for him. Three chariots were brought out; in the first sat Candragomin; in the second, Candrakirti and in the third was placed the image of Manjusri (the god of learning according to the Mahāyāna mythology), then followed the community of monks. The procession, thus arranged, passed through the town.

While in South India, Candragomin had composed a commentary on Pānini. He heard of a similar work by Candrakirti in Nālanda. Thinking his own work unnecessary, he threw it into a well, from whence it was afterwards recovered, as it was considered superior to Candrakirti's.

From Tibetan sources we know that Candragomin flourished early in tho eighth century, as he was the contemporary of Sīlā (son of Harsa) who reigned about A.D. 700.

He composed no less than sixty books on Buddhism in Sanskrit. His influence on Tibetan Buddhism was equal to that of Dipaṁkara or Abhayakara Gupta. As he was a devotee of the Goddess Tārā, he composed some books in praise of Her. He was a great grammarian as well and his works on grammar are read by many in Tibet. All his works were translated into Tibetan. Through them he was able to preach the doctrines of Lord Buddha. These works are his :

'Tārā-bhattārikāntara-bali-vidhi.'[1]
'Dêsnāṣṭava.'[2]
'Bhagavadārya-mañjusri-sādhistāna-sṭuṭi.'[3]
'Aryā-moghapāsa-pañca-deva-sṭoṭra.'[4]
'Manoharakalpa-nāma-lokanātha-sṭoṭra.'[4]
'Mahā-kāruṇika-sṭoṭra.'[5]
'Arya-mahā-kāruṇika-paridêvana-sṭoṭra.'[6]
'Aryāvalokitêsvara-sṭoṭra.'[6]
'Siṁha-nāda-sādhana.'[7]
'Arya-vajra-vidāraṇī-piṇdî-kṛta-sādhana.'[8]
'Arya-sitātapatrāparājitānāmopāyika.'[9]

[1] *Catalogue du Fond tibétain*, II, p. 124.
[2] *Ibid.*, II, p. 11.
[3] ,, p. 301.
[4] ,, p. 302.
[5] ,, p 303.
[6] ,, p. 304.
[7] ,, p. 321.
[8] ,, p. 331.
[9] ,, p. 359.

'Arya-sitātapatrāparājitānāmopākikā-blai-vidhi.'[1]

'Arya-tathāgatosnîsa-sîtātapatrāparājitā-pratyaṅgirā-nāmadhāranî-sādhana.'[1]

'Raksācakra.'[1]

'Yantra-vandhana.'[1]

'Akāla-maraṅa-nivāranopāya.'[1]

'Vighna-nivāraka-pramathanopāya.'[1]

'Camūdhvaṁsanopāya.'[2]

'Sidhi-sādhana.'[2]

'Bhaya-trāṅopāya.'[2]

'Karakaraksopāya.'[2]

'Kustacikiṭsopāya.'[2]

'Bali-vidhi.'[2]

'Arya-tathāgatosṅīsa-sîtātapatrāparājitā-pratyaṅgirā-nāma-dhāraṇī-sadhana.'[2]

'Arya-tathāgatosṅīsa-sītātapatrāparājitā-pratyaṅgirā-nāma-dhāraṅī-vidhi-nāma.'[2]

'Javra-rakṣā-vidhi.'[2]

'Pasu-mārī-rakṣā-vidhi.'[2]

'Santi-homa.'[2]

'Abhicāra karman.'[2]

'Pustī basi homa.'[2]

'Sidhi-sādhanānusārêna-mṛtabatsa-cikitṣā.'[2]

[1] *Catalogue du Fond tibétain*, II, p. 360.
[2] *Ibid.*, II, p. 361.

'Nivaraṅalavāka-vidhi.'[1]
'Caitya-sādhana-vidhi-krama-nāma.'[1]
'Bhagavatyu-srîsa-vijaya-sṭoṭra.'[2]
'Saṁjñiptā-sri-jambhala-sādhana.'[3]
'Haya-grîva-sādhana.'[4]
'Aṣta-sata-sādhana.'[5]
'Āyu-vardhanî-tārā-kalpa.'[6]
'Sri-mahā-tārā-sṭoṭra-nāma.'[6]
'Ārya-tārā-sṭoṭra Dvādasa-gātha.'[6]
'Ārya-tārā-sṭoṭra Visvakarma-sādhana-nāma.'[6]
'Ārya-tārā-devi-sṭoṭra-puspa-mālā-nāma.'
'Ārya-tārā-devi-stava-nāma.'[7]
'Asta-bhaya-trātā-sṭoṭra.'[7]
'Aryāsta-bhaya-trātā-nāma-tārā-sādhana.'
'Arya-jambhala-sṭoṭra.'[8]
'Jāla-grantha-vṛtti.'[9]
'Arya-tārā-dîvi-sṭoṭra-muktikāmālā-nāmā.'[10]

1 *Catalogue du Fond tibétain*, II, p. 363.
2 *Ibid.*, II, p. 365.
3 " p. 60.
4 *Ibid.*, III, pp. 61—2.
5 " p. 70.
6 " p. 71.
7 " p. 72.
8 " p. 89.
9 " p. 148.
10 " p. 185.

Arya-tārā-dîvi-sṭoṭra.'[1]
'Arya-tārā-sṭoṭra-praṇidhāna-[siddhi] nama.'[1]
'Aryāsta-mahā-bhayottarā-tārā-stava.'[1]
'Sisya-lêkha.'[2]
'Lokānanda-nātaka-nāma.'[3]
'Candragomi-praṇidhāna-nāma.'[4]

He composed these works on grammar:

'Candra-vyākaraṇa-sutra-nāma.'[5]
'Vimsatyupasarga-vṛtti-nāma.'[6]
'Uṇādi.'[7]
'Cāndrasyoṅādê-vṛtti-nāma.'[8]
'Cāndra-vyākaraṇa-varna-sutra-vṛtti.'[9]

Of these sixty works, the greater number belong to what is called in the Chinese Tripitaka, the Dhāranî section. The Chinese Tripitaka contains a considerable number of them, mostly

[1] *Catalogue du Fond tibétain*, III, p. 186.
[2] „ pp. 343 and 428.
[3] „ p. 418.
[4] „ p. 526.
[5] „ p. 457.
[6] „ p. 458.
[7] „ p. 507.
[8] „ p. 508.
[9] „ p. 512. This work of his inspired Rāma Candra to write another book on Pānini (III, p. 519).

translated into Chinese by Indian monks. In Tibetan Buddhist literature also these Dhāranî books found their place. Books like 'Rakṣā-cakra' or 'Akāla-maraṇa-nivāranopāya' are nothing but Dhāraṇis. We can include them in the Tantric group. They originated from the pen of Candragomin, but were introduced into Tibet later on, as they were translated. This Tāntricism influenced the Tibetans in a great measure. When this Buddhist Tāntricism made a compromise with the native *Bon* religion of Tibet, a new kind of Buddhism sprang up. That new phase of development came to be known as Lamaism. All sorts of sorcery, magic charms, spells, and mystic utterances like *Oṁ Maṇi Padmē Om* found a place in Tibetan Buddhism.

(5.)

SĀNTA RAKSITA

It was in the seventh century A.D. that Buddhism penetrated into Tibet during the reign of the King-sroṅ-tsan-gampo. He tried his best to make the teachings of Lord Buddha known to his subjects by inviting Indian pandits to his kingdom. For these efforts of his and of his two queens, all three are worshipped as Bodhisattvas by the Tibetans.

In the eighth century, there came another king to the throne of Tibet, whose name was Khri-sroṅ-deu-tsan. He was born in A.D. 728 and died in A.D. 864. He was a great patron of Buddhism and invited several Indian pandits to his court to propagate Buddhism in his kingdom. It was he who invited Acārya Sānta Raksita to Tibet.[1]

Sānta Raksita was born during the reign of King Gopala, who reigned up to A.D. 705. Perhaps he descended from the royal family

[1] Waddell's *Lamaism*, p. 28. Vidyabhusan's *Indian Logic*, etc., pp. 124—129.

of Zahor (in Bengal?). Before he proceeded to Tibet, he was staying in the University of Nālanda as a professor. He was one of the prominent pandits of the time, and belonged to the Svatantra Mādhyamika school. The Tibetan king, Khri-sroṅ-deu-tsan, hearing of his great learning, invited him to his court. When Sānta Raksita approached Tibet, ministers of the king came with an army to escort him to the royal palace singing songs of welcome.

In Tibet he began in right earnest the work of the propagation of the Buddhist faith. Acting on his advice, the king constructed the first Buddhist monastery in Tibet, namely, the monastery of Sam-ye, in A.D. 749. This new monastery was built after the model of the Odantapura Vihāra of Magadha. It was quite in the fitness of things that Ācārya Sānta Raksita should be appointed first abbot of this new vihāra. After working for a period of thirteen years in Tibet, Sānta Raksita breathed his last in A.D. 762. As a recognition of his work for the cause of Buddhism he became known in Tibet as Ācārya Bodhisattva. His name in Tibetan was Shi-wa-htsho.

He composed these two books: 'Vāda-Nyāya-vṛtti-vipañcitārtha,' which is a commentary on the 'Vāda-nyāya' of Dharma Kirti, and 'Taṭṭva-saṁgraha-kārikā'.

(6.)

PADMASAMBHAVA

On the advice of his *guru*, Sānta Raksita, the Tibetan king Khri-sroṅ-deu-tsan sent an invitation to another great Indian pandit, Padmasambhava of Nālanda. The account of this Indian pandit has been preserved in several Tibetan books and from them we know that he was the son of the King of Udyāna (Kasmira) named Indrabodhi. A story is told about his birth. At the death of the only son of King Indrabodhi, the whole kingdom became afflicted with grief. Conditions in the kingdom also became bad and the subjects began to pray to Lord Buddha for deliverance.

One day the king dreamt that he held a *vajra* in his hand. The next day, his priest told him that the saviour of the kingdom was born on a lotus in a certain tank. The king went to that tank and saw a child on a lotus. He asked him: "Who are you?" The boy answered: "I have come at the command of Lord Buddha." The king took the boy to his palace and brought him up as his own son. He was named Saroruha Vajra. (From this story he got his later name, Padmasambhava.) As the boy grew up, he shunned all pleasures and festivities. Once the prince killed some of the subjects, who were the enemies of Buddhism. At this the subjects complained against the Prince to the king, who banished him from his kingdom. Exiled from the kingdom of Udyāna (Kashmira), the Prince travelled from one place to another and gained much knowledge. When he came to Lahore, the princess of that kingdom wanted to marry him, as she could find no other suitable husband for herself. Afterwards he was married to this princess, who was called Kumārī Devi.

This and many other stories are current about him in Tibet. When the call came to him from the Tibetan king, he was residing in the monastery of Nālanda. He was one of the prominent expounders of the Yogācārya school of Tāntricism. From Nālanda Vihāra, he proceeded to Tibet in A.D. 747.

He was cordially welcomed by the king and his people. He assisted Ācārya Sānta Raksita in the construction of the first great monastery of Tibet in Samye. Padmasambhava also introduced the Tantric element in Tibetan

Buddhism. The monasteries of Nālanda and Vikramasīlā were strongholds of Tantric Buddhism. Hence all the pandits coming from these Vihāras preached the same cult of Tantra in Tibet. When it was intermixed with the *Bon* religion, a new aspect of Buddhism grew up in Tibet, which we call Lamaism. At first the orthodox followers of the *Bon* religion tried to oust Buddhism from Tibet. But as the Tibetans liked the spells and charms of the Tantric cult and its peculiar doctrine, it gradually occupied a pre-eminent position in Tibet, in spite of the protests of several learned men and ministers professing the *Bon* religion.

Buddhism had penetrated into China by the first century A.D. Buddhist monks, therefore, had begun to pour into Tibet propagating the doctrines of Buddha. These Chinese monks, however, sometimes came into conflict with the views propounded by Indian pandits. One such Chinese monk was Mahâyāna Hwa-shang, who found fault with the theories and doctrines preached by the royal *guru*, Sânta Raksita and Padmasambhava. Pandit Kamalasīla, who had reached Tibet by this time, invited him to a discussion. He was able to defeat and expel the Chinese monk from Tibet.

Pandit Padmasambhava is worshipped in Tibet in his Tantric manifestation. He is represented as wearing the dress of the Udyāna country (Kashmira). He has a *vajra* in his right hand and a human skull in the left. Under his armpit is a *trisula* piercing a human head. His two wives are seen standing, one on each side of him and offering wine and blood in a human skull. Thus in Tantric fashion Padmasambhava is represented and worshipped by his Tibetan followers.[1]

[1] *Vide* Waddel's *Lāmāism* about Padmasambhava.

He was the author of 'Samaya Paṅcasikā' which was translated by Bhiksu Ānandaprajṅa. He is known in Tibetan as Padmaḥbyuṅ-gnas-shabs (Ācārya Padmasambhavapāda).

(7.)

KAMALASĪLA

The same Tibetan king, Khri-sroṅ-deu-tsan, who invited Sānta Raksita and Padmasambhava, also asked Ācārya Kamalasīla to come to his court to help him in the propagation of the Buddhist faith in the country of Bhots.

Kamalasīla was also one of the famous professors of the Nālanda University. He was the contemporary of Sânta Raksita and Padmasambhava. He flourished somewhere between A.D. 728—786. Tantra was his special subject as a professor at Nālanda.

When he reached Tibet, a Chinese monk was speaking against the doctrines preached by Sānta Raksita and Padmasambhava. He invited Mahāyāna Hwa-shang, this Chinese Buddhist monk, to a discussion, defeated him and exiled him from Tibet.

Kamalasīla composed the following books on Mdo-hgrel (Sutra) in Sanskrit:

'Ārya-sapta-ṣatikā-prajñā-pāramitā-tîkā.'[1]
'Ārya-vajra-cchedikā-prajñā-pāramitatîka.'[2]
'Prajñā-pāramitā-hṛdaya-nāma-tîkā.'[3]
'Nyāya-bindu-pūrva-pakṣe-saṁkṣipta.'[4]
'Tattva-saṁgraha-pañjika.'[5]

(8.)

STHIRAMATI

The Chinese traveller Yuan Chwang speaks of Sthiramati as a scholar of Nālanda Vihāra and as associated with Guṇamati, one of the

[1] *Catalogue du Fond tibétain*, III, p. 287, translated into Tibetan by Upādhyāy Vimalamitra.

[2] *Ibid.*, III, p. 288, translated into Tibetan by Mañjusri and Jinamitra.

[3] „ p. 289, translated into Tibetan by Upādhyāya Kumāra-Sri-bhadra.

[4] Vidyabhusan's *Indian Logic*, etc., pp. 129—130.

[5] *Ibid.*

great Pusas of the time.[1] Sthiramati bore the title of Upādhyāya as well as of Ācārya.

Srimad Sthiramati seems to have been the disciple and spiritual descendant of Vajradhvaja, the master of Coṇ. He himself belonged to the country of Dpaṅ. He worked with his spiritual *guru* and finished the translation of a work called 'Vṛtta-mālā-stuti,' which had been begun by his *guru*.[2]

Sthiramati was known to the Tibetans as a great interpreter. He knew Tibetan well and translated many Sanskrit books into Tibetan. He was also famous as a grammarian and translated many books on grammar into that language. He was particularly familiar with the kalāpa system of Sanskrit grammar. It was under his auspices that the book 'Dhātu-sutra' was translated by Bodhisikhara into Tibetan.[3]

[1] Watters on *Yuan Chuang*, Vol. II, p. 109.
[2] *Ibid.*, III, p. 467.
[3] „ p. 506.

From Tibetan books we learn that Sthiramati lived at the temple of Tārābhaṭṭārikā at Nālanda in Magadha, the centre of science. There he translated the book, 'Ārya-manju-sri-nāma-saṁgîti-tîkā vimalaprabhā,' by Puṇḍarika.[1]

Sthiramati was the author of the following books:

'Prakarana-tîkā-visêsa-vyākhyā-nāma.'[2]
'Bodhi-ciṭṭa-druma.'[3]
'Pramālaṁkāra-visva-patala-vyuha.'[3]
'Samayāstāviṁsa-mūla-vṛṭṭi.'[4]
'Prakaraṇa-tîkā-vyākhyā.'[5]
'Arya-mahā - ratna - kuta - dharma-paryāya-sata - sāhasrika - parivarta - kāsyapa-parivarta-tika.'[6]
'Madhyānta-vibhanga-tîkā.'[7]

[1] *Catalogue du Fond tibétain*, II, p. 26.
[2] *Ibid.*, III, pp. 139—9.
[3] ,, p. 139.
[4] ,, p. 151.
[5] ,, p. 158.
[6] ,, p. 369.
[7] ,, p. 377.

'Paṇca-skandha-prakarana-baibhāsya.'[1]
'Parmālamkāra-viswa-patala-vyuha-nāma.'[2]

As he was a great Tibetan scholar, he preached the doctrines of Lord Buddha through his Tibetan rendering of the following seven books:

'Sri-vasudārā-sṭoṭra.'[3]
'Chiṇṇa-muṇḍā-vajra-yoginî-sādhana-nāma.'[4]
'Adhikāra-samgraha-nāma.'[5]
'Kalāpa-sutra-vṛṭṭi-nāma.'[6]
'Sambandhoḍḍêsa.'[7]
'Syāḍyanṭa-prakryā.'[8]
'Ṣisyahitā-kalāpa-sutra-vṛṭṭi.'[9]

Perhaps he was more learned in Tibetan than some of the Indian pandits, for he

[1] *Catalogue du Fond tibétain*, III, p. 387.
[2] *Ibid.*, II, p. 290.
[3] *Ibid.*, III, p. 80.
[4] „ p. 117.
[5] „ p. 459.
[6] „ p. 461.
[7] „ p. 460.
[8] „ p. 462.
[9] „ p. 505.

undertook the revision and correction of the following Tibetan versions:

'Saḍaṅga-yoga' by Mahā Pandit Vibhuti Candra.[1]

'Guṇa-bharaṅî-nāma-saḍaṅga-yoga-tippani.'[1]

'Lakṣanābhidhānodhṛta-laghu-tantra-piṇḍārtha-vivarana nāma.'[2]

'Vajra-pada-sārasaṁgraha-paṅjikā.'[3]

'Sri-buddha-kapāla-mahā-tantra-rāja-tîkā-abhayapadhati-nāma.'[4]

'Sri-madvimala-prabhâ-tantrāvataraṇa-vāda-hṛdayā-loka.'[5]

'Sêkoḍḍêsa-tippaṇî.'[6]

'Sri-sambaroḍaya-mahā-tantra-rājasya paṅjikā-padminî-nāma.'[7]

'Sri-sambaroḍaya-sādhana.'[8]

'Sri-swasaparno-lokêsvara-vistara-sādhana.'[9]

[1] *Catalogue du Fond tibétain*, II, p. 23.
[2] *Ibid.*, II, p. 27.
[3] „ p. 68
[4] „ p. 107.
[5] „ p. 16.
[6] „ p. 24.
[7] „ p. 31.
[8] „ p. 50.
[9] „ p. 322.

(9.)

BUDDHA KIRTI

Buddha Kirti was also associated with the University of Nālanda. He was a good Tibetan scholar and translated into Tibetan a Tantric book named 'Sri-samputa-tantra-rāja-tīka Amnāya-mañjarî-nāma,' which was originally composed by Mahāpanditā Abhayākara Gupta of Magadha[1] at the University.

Buddha Kirti was a colleague of Mahāpanditā Abhayākara Gupta of Vikramasīlā Vihāra, who flourished towards the end of the eleventh century and the beginning of the twelfth century A.D. He helped Abhayākara Gupta of Magadha in translating the book, 'Vajra-yānāpaṭṭi-mañjarî-nāma,' into Tibetan.[2] He was known to the Tibetans by the name of Saṅs-rgyas-grags-pa, (Buddha-Kirti)

[1] *Catalogue du Fond tibétain*, II, p. 71.

[2] *Ibid.*, II, p. 255.

and bore the titles of Bahusruta and Paiṇḍapātika.

FIVE MINOR PANDITS OF NĀLANDA

There are five other minor pandits belonging to the University of Nālanda. We find their names in the catalogue of the Tibetan Tripitaka as the authors or translators of some Buddhist books. We do not get much detailed information about their lives. They helped in the development of Tibetan Buddhism by their works. There is no need to belittle the influence exercised by them, personally or through their books, on Tibetan Buddhism. They gave of their best to Tibet.

(10.)

KUMĀRA SRI

The first of these monks was Mahāyogin Kumāra Sri of Nālanda. While he was residing in this University, he composed a Buddhistic work in Sanskrit. It is entitled 'Svādhisthāna-kramopadêsaka-sādhana'.[1] The original Sanskrit version is lost, but the Tibetan translation of this book (as in the case of other translations) still exists. The name of the Tibetan translator, through whose instrumentality we now possess the Tibetan version, is not known to us.

There was another monk bearing the same name, Kumāra Sri, who perhaps did not belong to the Nālanda Vihāra. This second Kumāra Sri was only an interpreter in Tibetan. He helped Mahāpandit Vanaratna of Eastern India in translating 'Aryābalokitêsvarasya-carpatiracitasṭoṭra'.[2]

(11.)
KARNAPATI

The second minor monk was Karnapati of the Nālanda Vihāra. He was a Tibetan

[1] *Catalogue du Fond tibétain*, II, p. 52.
[2] *Ibid.*, II, p. 303.

scholar and by his Tibetan rendering of 'Mahāyāna Lakṣaṇa-samuccaya [nâma]' he made this volume accessible to the Tibetan Buddhists. The book was originally written in Sanskrit by Ācārya Buddha-jñāña-pāda and was rendered into Tibetan at the University of Nālandā.

Karnapati bore both the titles of Upādhyāya and Paṇḍita.

(12 & 13.)

KARṄA SRI AND SŪRYADHVAJA

These two monks belonged to the monastery of Nālanda. They worked together, but we do not know when they flourished. Two translations were ascribed to them: 'Sri-rakta-yamāri-sādhana-nâma'[1] and 'Traidhakāya-vāka-chittádhisthānopadêsa-nāma'.[2]

Both these works were originally written in Sanskrit by Ācārya Buddha-jñāña-pāda.

[1] *Catalogue du Fond tibétain*, III, p. 168.
[2] *Ibid.*, III, p. 169.

Karṇa Sri and his colleague Sūryadhvaja were the first to translate them into Tibetan (at the Vihāra of Nālanda). They were afterwards translated into Tibetan by Ananda Bhadra.

(14.)

SUMATI SENA (SĪLĀ)

The last of these monks was Sumati Sena, who was also known as Sumati Sīlā. He resided at the great Vihāra of Sri Nālanda for a long time. While he was there, he composed in Sanskrit a book entitled 'Karma-siddha-tīkā,'[1] which was rendered into Tibetan by Visuddha Simha of India.

Sumati Sena was known in Tibetan as Blo-bzaṅ-ṅaṅ-Tshul. The Vihāra of Nālanda where he resided was called, in Tibetan, Dpal Nālendra (Sri Nālanda).

We should not confound him with Sumati-kirti, who revised the Tibetan translation of

[1] *Catalogue du Fond tibétain*, III, p. 389.

'Nyāya-bindu-tîkā'[1] or with the pandit Sumati, who translated 'Pramāna-vārtikālaṁkāra-tīkā'.[2]

---

[1] Vidyabhusan's *Indian Logic*, etc., p. 131

[2] *Ibid.*, p. 141.

CHAPTER V

PANDITS OF JĀGADDALA UNIVERSITY

THE monastery of Jāgaddala was one of the centres of culture in Bengal. It was founded by the King Rama Pala, who reigned over Bengal and Magadha from A.D. 1084—1130. The historical epic *Rāmacarita* speaks of the Jāgaddala Mahāvihāra, which was situated in the new capital city of Rāmapāla.[1] King Rāma Pāla founded the new city of Rāmāvati on the banks of the rivers Ganges and Karatoyā in the country of Varendra[2] which is identified with Northern Bengal. In that

[1] *Ramacarita*—MM. H. P. Sastri, Ch. 3. 5. 7. M.A.S.B., Vol. III, p. 47.
[2] *Ibid.*, p. 14.

beautiful capital, King Rāmapāla constructed a new vihāra which was called Jāgaddala Mahāvihāra. So we can place the date of the foundation of this new vihāra at the beginning of the twelfth century A.D. This university flourished only for a century, till the Muhammadan invasion of Bengal in A.D. 203.

During its life of a century it produced many learned scholars and pandits. The account of these monks, however, is very meagre. The Tibetan Tripitaka has preserved for us the names of some of the pandits of this great university, as well as the names of the works produced by those scholars.

The site of this vihāra, which Tibetans called by the name of Jāgadhala (Jāgaddala), has not yet been located. The *Rāmacarita* and the Tibetan books place it in the country of Varendra (Northern Bengal). Mr. A. K. Maitra is inclined to place it in the district of Dinajpur. Until the sites of Dinajpur are excavated and traces leading to the identification of the site are forthcoming, the question must be left undecided.

The pandits of Jāgaddala University were: Vibhuticandra, Dânasila, Subhākara and Moksakaragupta.

(1.)

VIBHUTICANDRA

One of the great scholars of the University of Jāgaddala was Vibhuticandra. He was a great Tibetan scholar and translated many Sanskritic Buddhist books into Tibetan. It seems probable that he visited Tibet, because we find that he chose Diṅ-Ri as the place for the Tibetan translation of 'Saḍaṅga-yoga-nāma' by Mahāpandita Anupamaraksita.[1] Where is this Diṅ-Ri? It is a plateau of Southern Tibet. If he translated that book at Diṅ-Ri, he must have visited Tibet. We find him

[1] Cordier's *Catalogue du Fond tibétain*, p. 19.

translating another book at the same place, Dpal Diṅ-Ri, called 'Sri-Kāla-cakropadesa-surya-candrasādhana-nāma'.[1]

Vibhuticandra bore the title of Mahāpandita. He perhaps studied under Sri Sābarisvara, who explained to him the book named 'Saḍaṅga-yoga-nāma'.[2] Vibhuticandra afterwards translated this Sanskrit book into Tibetan.

There is a popular book of the Buddhists, named, 'Jṅāṅa-cakṣuh-sādhana-nāma' which passed through the hands of several masters before it came to our monk Vibhuticandra. The book was originally composed by Ācārya Kālapāda, who explained it to Mahākāruṇika, that is, to Avalokitesvara and other Bodhisattvas. It was afterwards transmitted to Jṅāṅaḍāka, Surya Dharma, Ratnasribhadra, Sākyasribhadra, and lastly to Vibhuticandra.

[1] Cordier's *Catalogue*, p. 20.

[2] *Ibid.*, p. 21.

Here we find Vibhuticandra's name coupled with that of Sākyasribhadra. It supplies us with a clue as to the age in which Vibhuticandra flourished. Sākyasribhadra was, perhaps, the predecessor or contemporary of Vibhuticandra. We know that in A.D. 1203, at the time of the invasion of Vikramasīlā by Bakhtiyar Khilji, Sākyasribhadra was the head of the Vikramasīlā Vihāra. Perhaps Vibhuticandra flourised at the same time, before the Moslem invasion. After the destruction of the Vikramasīlā University, Sākyasribhadra visited the University of Jāgaddala. We do not know whether Sakyasribhadra met him there; but it seems probable that he accompanied Sākyasribhadra to Tibet, because, after the coming of the Moslems to Bengal and Magadha, the Buddhist culture slowly died away under their persecutions. Vibhuticandra, therefore, flourished just on the eve of the Moslem attack of Magadha and Bengal.

He was a great Tibetan scholar and translated numerous Sanskrit books into Tibetan. These translations are :

'Saḍaṅga-yoga-nāma.'[1]
'Saḍanga-yoga-tîkā.'[2]
'Sri-kāla-cakropadesa-surya-candra-sādhana-nāma.'[2]
'Jṅāṅa-cakṣuḥ-sādhana-nāma.'[2]
'Saḍaṅga-yoga-nāma.'[3]
'Saḍaṅga-yoga.'[4]
'Guṇa-bharaṅi-nāma-saḍaṅga-yoga-tippaṅī.'[5]
'Luhi-pādābhisamaya-vṛtti-saṁvarodaya-nāma.'[6]
'Luhi-pādābhi-samaya-tīkā-visâsḍyota-nāma.'[6]
'Sri-samvara-maṅḍala-vidhi.'[6]
'Vajra-satva-sādhana-nibandha.'[7]

[1] *Catalogue du Fond tibétain*, II, p. 19.
[2] *Ibid.*, II, p. 20.
[3] ,, p. 21.
[4] ,, p. 23. (Corrected by Sthiramati.)
[5] ,, p. 23.
[6] ,, p. 49.
[7] ,, p. 138.

'Paṅca-krama-mata-ṭîkā.'[1]
'Manju-vajra-pujā-vidhi.'[2]
'Raktāri-catuha-sakti-prathaka-sādhana'[3]
'Ārya-sita-tāpatrāparājitā-sādhana'[4]
'Guru-sādhana'[5]
'Āryā-mogha-pāṣa-sādhana.'[6]
'Guru-siddhi.'[7]

Vibhuticandra composed the following books in Sanskrit and himself translated them into Tibetan :

'Antar-maṅjarî-nāma.'[8]
'Svapnohana.'[9]
'Tri-saṁbara-prabhā-mālā-nāma.'[10]
'Vajra-carcikā-karma-sādhana.'[11]

[1] *Catalogue du Fond tibétain*, II, p. 142.
[2] *Ibid.*, II, p. 156.
[3] „ p. 178.
[4] „ p. 365.
[5] *Ibid.*, III, p. 227.
[6] „ p. 178.
[7] „ p. 228.
[8] *Ibid.*, II, p. 21.
[9] „ p. 126.
[10] *Ibid.*, III, p. 85.
[11] „ p. 173.

'Āryā-mogha-pāṣa-sādhana.'[1]

'Bodhicaryāvatāra-tātparya-panjikā Vises-dyotanī-nāma.'[2]

(2.)

DĀNASILA

Mahāpandit Dānasila belonged to the famous University of Jāgaddala. He bore not only the titles of Mahāpandit, Pandit and Upādyāya, but also that of Ācārya. He knew Tibetan and translated several books from the Sanskrit. He translated a book called 'Kāka-caritra' into Tibetan at the Vihāra of Yar-kluṅs-thaṅ-po-che in Central Tibet, which shows that he visited Tibet.

Dānasila seems to have been associated with Jinamitra. They translated together four books:

'Siksā-samuccaya' of Sāntideva.[3]

'Āryā-vikalpa-pravesadhāraṇī-tīkā.'[4]

[1] *Catalogue du Fond tibétain*, III, p. 178.
[2] *Ibid.*, III,p. 310.
[3] „ p. 325.
[4] „ p. 366.

'Karma-prajñapti.'[1]
'Sāra-samuccaya-nāma Abhidharmāvatāra-tīkā.'[2]

Dānasila himself translated the following Sanskrit books into Tibetan:

'Mārîcyāḥ-sādhana.'[3]
'Sukla-caṇda-mahāroṣaṇa-sādhana.'[4]
'Āryā-cala-sādhana.'[4]
'Ārya-mañju-sri-sādhana.'[5]
'Manohara-kalpa-nāma-loka-nātha-sṭoṭra.'[6]
'Rakta-yamāri-mantra-saṁgraha-nāma.'[6]
'Rakta-yamāri-karmā-bali-sādhana Cinṭā-maṇi-nāma.'[6]
'Rati-priyā-sādhana-nāma.'[6]
'Yakṣa-nata-natî-sādhana.'[6]
'Yakṣiṇî-pārthivî-lakṣmî-sādhana.'[6]
'Yakṣa-nandikara-sādhana.'[7]

[1] *Catalogue du Fond tibétain*, p. 393. (Assisted by Prajñāvarma also.)
[2] *Ibid.*, III, p 398.
[3] *Ibid.*, II, p. 386.
[4] ,, p. 357. (He was the author of these two books.)
[5] ,, p. 302.
[6] ,, p. 183.
[7] ,, p. 184.

'Yakṣa-rāja-kîlikîla-sādhana.'[1]
'Pîḍana-mahâ-yakṣa-sênāpati-sādhana.'[1]
'Srî-candra-dêvînāma-sādhana.'[1]
'Kuṇḍala-dhāraṇî-hārîti-sādhana.'[1]
'Ratna-mālā.'[1]
'Nāgî-sādhana.'[1]
'Nāgî-basu-pālā-mukhî-nāma-sādhana.'[1]
'Nāgyā-phunāmopāya.'[2]
'Manoharî-sādhana.'[2]
'Subhayā sādhana.'[2]
'Visāla-nêtrî-sādhana.'[2]
'Rati-rāga-sādhana.'[2]
'Aparājitā-nāma-sādhana.'[2]
'Adhijayājitā-sādhana.'[2]
'Purṇa-bhadrā-sādhana.'[2]
'Bhutî-sundarî-sādhana.'[3]
'Sri-jaya-suṇdarî-sādhana.'[3]
'Vimala-suṇdarî-sādhana.'[3]
'Pisāca-pilupāla-sādhana.'[3]
'Pisāca-maṅidhara-sādhana.'[3]
'Kṛsna-pisāca-sādhana.'[1]
'Pisāca-kṛsna-sāra-sādhana.'[3]

[1] *Catalogue du Fond tibétain*, III, p. 184.

[2] *Ibid.*, II, p. 185.

[3] „ p. 186.

'Pisācî-hanā-sādhana.'[1]
'Ālukā-nāma sādhana.'[1]
'Alaguptā-nāma-sādhana.'[1]
'Khara-mukhī-sādhana.'[1]
'Āhumbinî-pisācî-sādhana.'[2]
'Ucchusmānāma-sādhana.'[2]
'Kṣukṣu-srî-kundalî-sādhana.'[2]
'Pisācî-karṇa-gṛhyā-sādhana.'[2]
'Pisācî-krṣna-mukhî-sādhana.'[3]
'Yamāri-ciṇtāmaṇi-mālā-nāma-sādhana.'[3]
'Rakta-yamāri-sādhana.'[4]
'Yamāri-yantrā-vali.'[5]
'Rakta-yamāri-sādhana.'[6]
'Suklaika-jatā-sādhana.'[7]
'Aka-jatā-sādhana.'[8]
'Arya-vajra-tārā-sādhana.'[9]
'Abhisamaya-mañjarî.'[10]

[1] *Catalogue du Fond tibétain*, III, p. 187.
[2] *Ibid.*, III, p. 187.
[3] *Ibid.*, II, p. 188.
[4] ,, p. 179.
[5] ,, p. 177.
[6] ,, p. 176.
[7] ,, p. 122.
[8] ,, p. 121.
[9] ,, p. 94.
[10] ,, p. 63.

'Yogānusārinî-nāma-vajra-yoginî-tîkā.'[1]
'Sri-mañju-vajrādi-kramābhisamaya-smuccaya-nispanna-yogāvali-nāma.'[2]
'Hasta-bāla-prakaraṅa-kārikā.'[3]
'Kāka-caritra.'[4]

He must be regarded as a great translator for he translated no less than fifty-four books into Tibetan without aid, and four more with the help of Jinamitra. These books had a great influence on Tibetan Buddhism. His work in the field of Buddhism may be compared to that of Dipaṁkara or of Abhayakaragupta. He wrote only one book in Sanskrit, 'Dhyāna-saḍa-dharma-vyavasthāna-vṛitti'.[5]

(3.)

SUBHAKARA

The third scholar associated with the Jāgaddala University was Subhakara. He is

[1] *Catalogue du Fond tibétain*, II, p. 59.
[2] *Ibid.*, III, p. 230.
[3] " p. 297.
[4] " p. 486.
[5] " p. 320.

sometimes spoken of as Sumbhakara. Subhakara bore the title of Pandit. He was the spiritual guide (*guru*) of Sākya Sri, who was perhaps the same monk as Sākyasribhadra of Kashmir, the abbot of Vikramasīlā Vihāra (before 1203), so Pandit Subhakara must have flourished a little before the Moslems attacked and ravaged the country.

While he was residing in the Vihāra of Jāgaddala, he composed a Buddhistic book in Sanskrit named 'Siddhāika-vîra-tantra-tîkā'.[1] It was translated into Tibetan by Ācārya Dānasila.

(4.)

MOKṢĀKARAGUPTA

The last monk belonging to the great Vihāra of Jāgattala (Jāgaddala) was Mokṣākaragupta. He was a good logician of the Buddhist school. He wrote a book on logic,

[1] *Catalogue du Fond tibétain*, II, p. 293.

named 'Tarka-bhāsā,' which was translated into Tibetan by Bhikshu Srimat Sthiramati of Dpaṅ, which thus reached Tibet.

Mokṣākaragupta bore the titles of Mahā-pandita and Bhikshu. His name in Tibetan was Thar-paḥi-ḥbyuṅ-gnas-kyisbas-pa.

These four pandits of the Jāgaddala University tried their very best to develop Tibetan Buddhist literature by their numerous translations. Their ideas and their doctrines permeated Tibet through their books and by direct preaching.

(5.)

A Pandit of Odantapuri

Another seat of learning in Magadha was Odantapuri, which is known in Tibetan as Hphur-byed-kyi-groṅ-khyer. It is difficult to identify the exact site of Odantapuri.

We know of only one pandit of this Vihāra, Prabhākara of Chadtrapur—which is perhaps Chatarpur in Bengal. He translated 'Sāmudrika-vyañjanu-varnana' into Tibetan.[1]

According to the writer of 'Universities in Ancient India,' the Vihāra of Odantapuri was established long before the Pāla dynasty came into power in Magadha.[2] It was situated near Pataliputra. It is unfortunate we have no detailed information about this vihāra. The Pāla kings endowed this monastery with a splendid library of Brahmanical and Buddhistic works.

The vihāra accommodated numerous students, who came there from various parts of India. When Pandit Abhayakara Gupta was at the head of the Buddhist hierarchy in Magadha (that is towards the end of the eleventh and the beginning of the twelfth century A.D.), there were no less than one thousand Buddhist monks at the University of Odantapuri, as compared to three thousand monks at

[1] *Catalogue du Fond Tibétain*, III, p. 484.

[2] *Universities in Ancient India*. Journal of the Buddhist Text and Research Society, Vol. VII, Part IV, p. 21 (1906).

the Vikramasīlā Vihāra and a thousand more at Vajrāsana (*i.e.*, Buddha Gaya).[1]

The building of the monastery of Odantapuri was magnificient. It was taken as a model by the Tibetan Buddhists. When the Tibetan King Khri-sroṅ-deu-tsan was constructing a Buddhist monastery at Sam-ye in A.D. 749, he built it after the model of the monastery of Odantapuri on the advice of his Indian *guru*, Sānta Raksita, who had proceeded to Tibet at the invitation of the Tibetan King.

NAMES AND DATES OF PANDITS

I. Pandits of Vikramasīlā :

1. Buddha Jṅaṅapāda (8th cent. A.D.).
2. Vairocana Raksita (8th cent. A.D.).
3. Jelāri (10th cent. A.D.).
4. Prajṅā Karamati.
5. Ratnākara Sānti.
6. Jṅāṅa Sri Mitra.
7. Ratna Vajra.
8. Vāgisvara Kirti.

(4–8: 10th cent).

[1] S. C. Das—J.A.S.B., 1882, pp. 1—18.

9. Dipaṁkara } (980—1053).
10. Virya Simha }
11. Abhayakaragupta (11th—12th cent.).
12. Tathāgata Raksita.
13. Ratna Kirti (10th cent. A.D.).
14. Manjusri.
15. Dharma Kirti.
16. Sākya-Sri-Bhadra (—1203).

II. Pandits of Nālanda :

1. Arya Deva (4th cent.).
2. Silabhadra (c. A.D. 585—640).
3. Dharmapâla (—A.D. 600).
4. Candragomin (8th cent.).
5. Sānta Raksita }
6. Padma Sambhava } (c. 715—762).
7. Kamalasila }
8. Sthiramati.
9. Buddha Kirti.
10. Kumāra Sri.
11. Kamapati.
12. Karna Sri }
13. Suryadhvaja }
14. Sumati Sena (Sila).

III. Pandits of Jāgaddala :

1. Vibhuticandra } (—1203).
2. Dānasila }
3. Subhākara.
4. Moksakaragupta.

IV. Pandit of Odantapuri :

1. Prabhakara.

BIBLIOGRAPHY

1. W. W. Rock Hill: 'Life of Buddha' (London, 1884).
2. Grünwedel: 'Mythologie du Buddhism en Tibet et en Mongolie' (Leipzig, 1900).
3. Gethy: 'Gods of Northern Buddhism.'
4. B. H. Hodgson: 'Illustrations of the Literature and Religion of the Buddhists' (Serampore, 1841).
5. L. A. Waddel: 'The Buddhism of Tibet or Lamaism' (1895).
6. L. A. Waddel: 'Description of Lhāsa Cathedral' (J. A. S. B., 1895).
7. R. L. Mitra: 'The Sanskrit Buddhist Literature of Tibet.'
8. H. Cordier: 'Bibliotheca Sinica' (Paris, 1904).

9. P. Cordier: 'Catalogue du Fond tibétain' (Paris, 1914).

10. B. Nanjio: 'A Catalogue of Chinese Translations of Buddhist Tripitaka' (Oxford, 1883).

11. Watters: 'On Yuan Chuang.'

12. Takakusu: 'It-sing.'

13. Schiefner: 'Târânātha's Geschichte des Buddhismus.'

14. A. Csoma de Körös: 'Tibetan Studies'. (Cal., 1912).

15. Legge: 'Travels of Fahien' (Oxford, 1886).

16. S. C. Vidyabhusan: 'History of the Mediæval School of Indian Logic' (Calcutta, 1909).

17. V. Smith: 'Early History of India' (Oxford, 1914).

18. S. C. Das: 'Indian Pandits in the Land of Snow' (Calcutta, 1893).

Printed by J. R. Aria at the Vasanta Press, Adyar, Madras.